THE FOUR DIMENSIONS OF AVERY BRUNDAGE

THE
FOUR DIMENSIONS
OF
AVERY BRUNDAGE

HEINZ SCHÖBEL

EDITION LEIPZIG

TRANSLATED FROM THE GERMAN BY JOAN BECKER

COPYRIGHT 1968 BY EDITION LEIPZIG

NO. 600/87/68

TYPOGRAPHY AND DESIGN: HORST ERICH WOLTER, LEIPZIG

PRODUCED BY OFFIZIN ANDERSEN NEXÖ, LEIPZIG

PRINTED IN GERMANY

PREFACE

THE author of this sketch has had many opportunities of meeting Avery Brundage and talking with him about sport, work and art. He does not claim to present a complete picture of the man, but he has tried to find an answer to the question often asked as to how Avery Brundage has been able to combine in his own person such widely different characteristics and interests.

First there is Avery Brundage the active sportsman who, starting at the bottom, achieved remarkable successes in a very short time and ended as All-Around Champion of the United States, a title which he held for several years.

Then there is Avery Brundage the sports leader who, after retiring from participation, climbed the administrative ladder rung by rung, held top functions in United States sport, attracted international attention, and finally, in 1952, was elected to the highest position in the world of amateur sport—that of President of the International Olympic Committee.

And then again there is Avery Brundage the energetic and successful construction engineer who, as a practical and inventive lad, made his own sports equipment and, later on, built huge steel and concrete structures and helped to determine the architectural appearance of the great city of Chicago. Here he emerges not only as a man who made his youthful dreams come true but also as a man who has always been true to his own maxim: "Never say die!", who refused to accept defeat in the international economic crisis of 1929 and led his apparently bankrupt business to new successes.

And finally there is Avery Brundage the art-lover and collector who, with admirable perseverance and consistency, has gathered together treasures of Asian art of a quality hardly to be found anywhere else and, at the height of his career, presented these treasures to the city of San Francisco and thus to the general public.

As an art-lover and collector he never tired of linking art and sport and urging that both be encouraged in conjunction. Where has he found the strength for all this? What is for him the connecting link? Text and pictures in the following pages stress Avery Brundage's activities as a leader of the Olympic Movement and as an art-lover and collector.

The author hopes that this book will encourage art and sports experts to study the various aspects of this complex field and to work out on this basis a thoroughly scientific presentation of the whole subject. From Avery Brundage's life emerges the main aim of the Olympic Games—to assure that mankind develops to a higher level through sport in a peaceful world.

Finally, the author wishes by means of this short biographical sketch to render IOC President Avery Brundage his thanks and the thanks of all people of good will, in connection with his 80th birthday, for all that he has accomplished for the Olympic Movement through his tireless activity and devotion.

The author thanks all those who assisted him with this book, and especially Professor René-Yvon Lefebvre d'Argencé, Director of the Avery Brundage Foundation in San Francisco. Thanks are equally due to Mr. Frederick J. Ruegsegger, Executive Assistant of the IOC President, for his help in clarifying questions and for securing illustrations.

Heinz Schöbel

AVERY BRUNDAGE was born in Detroit on September 28th 1887. His parents and the rest of the Brundage family moved to Chicago in 1893, the year of the famous World's Columbian Exposition, and he lived part of the time with aunts and uncles and grandparents. Thus at an early age, through varied relationships, he developed traits of character like independence in thought and action, energy, self-discipline and determination.

His school years, at the Chicago English High and Manual Training School, which set very high standards, were not easy; he had to travel six or seven miles to and fro each day, partly on foot. Brundage has often spoken of his good fortune in having excellent teachers there. Because of his eagerness to learn and the efforts he made, he was one of the top boys in his class. At the age of 14 he won a competition organised by the Hearst Press; the prize was a trip to Washington to see the inauguration of President McKinley. Later on, at the university, he was well ahead of his fellow-students in general knowledge. He studied civil engineering at the University of Illinois from 1905 to 1909, a course which at that time included classes in structural, electrical and mechanical engineering.

At college he had the same thirst for knowledge he had had at school, and he did not confine himself to his own subject. At high school he had edited the school magazine, and although he was an engineering student he was chosen to edit the Illinois University literary monthly. He belonged to a social fraternity, and was elected by three honorary organisations, membership in which was a high distinction. Admission to the first two of these honorary organisations was by recommendation of the teaching staff and to the third by his fellow undergraduates. Only students of outstanding academic achievement and personal character were selected.

Brundage's university career reveals the breadth of his interests; he studied his own subject, civil engineering, for three years, but in his fourth year he attended additional lectures in economics, philosophy, psychology, literature and aesthetics, because he believed that these would be of tremendous value in later life. He left the University in

1909 with a civil engineer's diploma and the degree of Bachelor of Science.

The desire to add steadily to his knowledge is a characteristic feature of his development which has determined his outlook all his life. Underlying this is the ideal of a broadly cultured personality in which professional work and a well-thought-out use of leisure supplement each other.

After finishing his studies Brundage gained a few years' experience as construction superintendent, first with a prominent architectural firm and then with an outstanding building enterprise, but already in 1915 at the age of 28 he had his own construction firm, the Avery Brundage Company, which expanded rapidly.

Brundage was not conscripted in the First World War, but was called to Washington to take charge of government building projects, so that he did not have to interrupt his professional career. As a builder he contributed substantially to the appearance of the city of Chicago after the war. The mammoth steel and concrete structures shooting up into the sky had always impressed him, and the Avery Brundage Company soon became responsible for the erection of imposing skyscrapers, warehouses, office buildings, factories and also bridges. For Henry Ford, for example, his firm built what was at that time the largest factory in Chicago on an area covering 16 acres.

The exertion of Brundage's physical and mental powers reached a culmination when the world-wide economic crisis brought ruin to many firms and banks in 1930 and a number of his clients also reached the end of their strength and their courage. Avery Brundage attributes to sport and his own traits of character the fact that his construction company remained solvent and was able to weather the crisis. Only his accountant knew that he went about the city with empty pockets. But since he had an excellent reputation, the banks retained their confidence in him and he was thus able to obtain the necessary credit.

During his successful business years Avery Brundage laid the foundations which enabled him later on to follow the inclinations awakened by his extremely varied studies. He was especially interested in sport and in art. He had collected stamps as a schoolboy and this had aroused his interest in the special features of other countries at an early age. As a young building engineer he had also embarked with friends upon an expedition into an unexplored part of the United States, and as he grew older he became more and more interested in getting to know other countries and their peoples. This also explains his tremendous interest in reading. Even as a boy he devoured every book he could lay his hands on—adventure stories, travel books and historical novels—and spent all his free time in museums. The Chicago Field Museum of Natural History, in which he devoted whole days at a time, gave him many new ideas. It is no exaggeration to say that Brundage is today familiar with nearly every important museum in the world. Despite all the work attached to his office as top representative of international sport, he always finds time to visit places where the treasures of art created by man are collected together and preserved.

As a result of his many activities, Brundage has won great public recognition and respect. He was and remains active in a variety of economic institutions. He was elected president of the Construction Division Association after the First World War. In 1949 the Chamber of Commerce of Santa Barbara awarded him the title of "Excelentísimo Señor Don" for his outstanding civic contribution. At the centenary celebration of Northwestern University he was awarded an honorary diploma "in recognition of the impress he has made upon his generation during a lifetime of distinguished service as a resident of one of the States which comprised the old Northwest Territory."

Four years later, in 1955, the George Williams College in Chicago presented him with its highest award, that of honorary Doctor of Law. On this occasion some important qualities in Avery Brundage were expressed in the following words: "He has consistently opposed those who would place skill above sportsmanship, fame above nobility, and success above honour."

In 1957 the city of Chicago, which celebrated the 120th anniversary of its establishment in that year, awarded him the newly founded Medal of Merit. On his part Avery Brundage has demonstrated his attachment to Chicago by presenting the city with a 100,000-dollar Olympic Memorial Fountain on his 80th birthday in September 1967.

9

"This gift... I hope, will stimulate... the further development of Chicago's beauty and growth as a cultural and recreational center," he said on that occasion.

A number of other honours should be mentioned here: the University of Illinois declared him an "outstanding alumnus" in 1958, and a portrait in oils with an appropriate inscription hangs in the entrance hall of the Student Union Building there. The Lincoln Academy of Illinois presented him with a Sports and Athletics award in 1965. Brundage has been made an honorary citizen of seven cities, including Tokyo and San Francisco. He has a great number of foreign decorations, including awards from France, Italy, Germany, Sweden, Finland, the Lebanon, Iran, San Marino, Mexico, Norway, Spain, Congo and Portugal. The Japanese presented him with the highest award ever given to foreigners, the Order of the Sacred Treasure, First Class.

This busy man, known and respected throughout the world, directs his extensive affairs from an office on the 18th floor of the La Salle Hotel, Chicago, which he has owned since 1941. He occupies three rooms there in the heart of one of the youngest large cities in the world. He has an apartment on Chicago's Gold Coast looking out over Lake Michigan. And in the charming city of Santa Barbara, California, on the Pacific Coast, far from the busy life of Chicago, he installed himself in a Spanish-style home surrounded by gardens to which Helen Comstock paid tribute in her book on the hundred most beautiful American homes. This was Brundage's pride until it burned down in a devastating forest fire just before the 1964 Olympic Games in Tokyo. Many extremely valuable art objects and treasured mementos were lost forever in the flames.

Brundage has in the meantime acquired a house in another part of Santa Barbara which his wife Elizabeth, an accomplished musician, whom he married in 1927, looks after with the same care which she gave to their former home. This is a two-story Mediterranean-style villa with a tower. Brundage's many duties permit him to spend no more than a few weeks a year there, for he is very much occupied by all the travelling he does on behalf of international sport and the world-wide Olympic Movement.

10

AVERY BRUNDAGE climbed the ladder to the Olympic heights rung by rung. When prominent American sportsmen joined together in 1888 to found the Amateur Athletic Union of the United States, very little public attention was paid to sport. But Brundage early in life, felt a compulsion for strenuous athletic competition. He was not deterred by the circumstance that he had to wear spectacles from the age of ten. The avenue for his sports career opened when Pierre de Coubertin insisted on the need for physical education and training, and revived the Olympic Games. It is an interesting fact that discus-throwing, one of the main disciplines in the ancient Olympic Games, played a part in Brundage's first exercises. Not that he had a standard discus to practice with; in his search for something suitable Brundage came across a large, flat washer and he used this as a discus. For the long jump all he needed was a sand-pit and for weight-putting a heavy stone. Later on, in manual training classes, he cast a standard shot and a hammer for himself and made some hurdles.

He was left to his own resources in all this, for the school—like most in that era—offered no encouragement; it had no gymnasium, no swimming-pool and no sports instructor. Practising was done in meadows and parks. To help improve his running, jumping and weight-throwing, he invented his own exercises which he could practise in his room when he got up or before going to bed. And when he had to take a letter to the post, for instance, or sweep up snow or run an errand, he put as much energy into it as if he were training for the next contest.

The difficulties, and finding ways to overcome them, certainly account for the strong feeling of self-reliance which he was already developing. Brundage says today that that time was very important in forming his character. It strengthened his will and built up his determination never to say die. At college he was one of those who joined together in sports groups and associations. He played basketball and football and was manager of the track team. He very quickly gained a reputation as a sportsman. In 1905, while still at the Chicago English High and Manual Training School, he was heralded as the "high school athlete find of the year." When he left college Brundage was discus champion of the "Big Ten," the ten leading universities of the Middle West, and he won a special medal for athletic achievement. He had so steeled himself by all-around training that he was used in the university contests as general utility man in several disciplines. This prepared him for victory in the All-Around Championships which he entered only after graduation. This included ten disciplines and called for enormous energy, muscular strength, endurance and general fitness. The All-Around Championships correspond in general to the present-day decathlon, but were tougher in that there was only a short rest of five minutes between each discipline. It was ten events in one afternoon. The immediate succession of the 100-yards race, putting the 16-pound shot, the running high jump, walking (half-mile), throwing the hammer (16 pounds), the pole vault, hurdle race (120 yards), weight-throwing (56 pounds), the long jump and the mile race is the most strenuous and difficult athletic test ever devised.

As a result of his success Avery Brundage was taken into the United States national team and sent to Stockholm to compete in the 1912 Olympic Games. He participated in both the decathlon and the pentathlon, but did not win a medal in this first international contest. His later development indicated that he was not yet at the top of his form. Nevertheless, his fifth place in the pentathlon at Stockholm encouraged him to continue training, and as a reward he became United States champion in the All-Around Championships in 1914, 1916 and 1918, as a member of the Chicago Athletic Association. This was at a time when he was working long hours to build up his steadily expanding business and could devote only his very limited free time to training. According to newspaper reports of that time he trained at night by moonlight after he had finished a busy day's work.

It is within the bounds of possibility that Brundage would have won medals or even an Olympic victory if the 1916 Olympic Games had not had to be cancelled because of the First World War. Characteristic of his attitude toward sport is a remark, published in the Chicago press at that time: "Not to develop the latent possibilities of the human body is a crime, since it certainly violates the law of nature."

In 1918 Brundage won the Helms World Trophy as All-Around Champion of the USA, a symbolic award for the highest single achievement in sport. In the same year he retired as unbeaten All-Around Champion, but this did not mean that he was turning his back on active sport. Handball, which is a court game not identical with European field handball, had in the meantime captured his interest and he soon gained the reputation of being one of the ten best players in the country in this sport, too. He also helped organise intra-city tournaments. The famous sprinter, Charles W. Paddock, whose career was just beginning when Brundage retired from competitive sport, once said of him: "I remember very distinctly that he was not so much a born athlete as he was a great fighter."

After ending his career as an active sportsman Avery Brundage began to take an interest in the administrative side of sport. He held many posts on a national level before he entered the international scene. He was chairman of the athletic committee of the Chicago Athletic Association, for example, and as chairman of the athletic committee of the Chicago Association of Commerce he contributed to the development of sport activities in all the important branches of industry. For many years he represented his university as a member and as president of the Alumni Board, which administered the sport activities of the above-mentioned "Big Ten" universities. Early in the 1920's he was president first of the central section and later of the National Amateur Athletic Union, which was then the most important amateur sports organisation of the United States. He exercised this function until 1936. In 1929 he took over the presidency of the United States Olympic Committee, which he held for twenty-four years.

The Amateur Athletic Union was responsible for the selection of United States Olympic candidates. But Brundage showed full understanding for the claim of the National Collegiate Athletic Association, which was in charge of university sports, to have a voice in the selection of those who were to compete in the Olympic Games. He showed diplomatic skill in reaching a suitable agreement on this and his far-sightedness in this instance did much to unite the various amateur sport bodies and keep peace for twenty-five years. An essential trait in

Brundage's character is revealed here; narrow-mindedness, jealousy and everything which might injure the cause of sport is foreign to him.

After exercising the function of president of the two most important United States sports organisations simultaneously for seven years, Brundage retired from the Amateur Athletic Union in 1936.

Brundage's work as head of the Olympic Movement in one of the world's leading sport countries soon attracted international attention. As a result he was elected vice-president of the International Amateur Athletic Federation in 1930, and later vice-president of the International Amateur Handball Federation and of the International Amateur Basketball Federation. In 1936 he became a member of the International Olympic Committee, and a year later was elected to its Executive Board.

Another high spot in his career was his election in 1940 by the countries of the Western hemisphere as first president of the Comité Deportivo Panamericano at a congress to organise the Pan American Games in Buenos Aires. In 1946 he became vice-president of the IOC and in 1952, during the Games of the XV Olympiad in Helsinki, the IOC elected him its fifth president. He is the first non-European to occupy this position. Since then he has been regularly and unanimously re-elected. This was a clear vote of confidence in the Olympic activities of a man who is regarded as the guardian and the promoter of the ideals of Baron Pierre de Coubertin.

Avery Brundage, active in the Olympic Movement for over half a century, has always supported the basic ideals of the great French educator and humanist, the founder of the modern Olympic Games, and he has stated this in almost every speech he has made. In his speech at the opening of the 64th IOC Session in Rome in 1966, he said: "His (Coubertin's) thoughts (of the Olympic Games) were on the comprehensive welfare of mankind and on the peace of the world, than which nothing can be more important... He knew there was a need to demonstrate that men of all kinds were entitled to be placed on the same footing and to have the same opportunities... He knew there was a need to demonstrate... the devotion to the cause rather than to the reward."

14

Like Coubertin, Brundage goes far beyond sports, in the narrow sense, in his evaluation of the Olympic idea. What Coubertin said in a radio talk about the philosophical foundations of modern Olympics has been interpreted in its essentials by Avery Brundage at IOC Sessions and on other occasions all over the world. Both agree in their evaluation of the fundamental elements of the Olympic idea.

Both Coubertin and Brundage stress, as the most important basic idea, that the outstanding value of the Games consists in bringing the youth of all nations together in friendly sports contests and helping them to know each other better. To apply this basic principle creatively means to put into practice the necessity of maintaining peace. It was therefore extremely important to have the Olympic idea take root in as many countries as possible. Coubertin lived to see how the thirteen nations which sent competitors to the 1896 Olympic Games increased to twenty-seven in 1912. Brundage has worked tirelessly to continue the spread of the Olympic Movement, and the number of countries competing has increased from Olympiad to Olympiad. He has been travelling around the world for many years in his efforts to draw more countries into the Olympic Movement, and there are now 125 National Olympic Committees recognized and eligible to participate in the Games. Statistics show that he sometimes covers more than 100,000 miles a year. He takes the view that the youth of all nations, regardless of their social systems, should cooperate in the Olympic Movement and measure their strength in peaceful contest at the Olympic Games.

Brundage had "visions of a happier and more peaceful world" when he watched competitors from ninety-four countries march into the stadium in Tokyo. He spoke of this with great satisfaction in his 80th birthday speech, "representatives of… every race, every color, every religion, every political affiliation… all united behind the handsome Olympic banner with its five multicolored circles." His attitude to the Olympic Movement and to the development of sport in the Soviet Union should also be understood from this point of view. He has followed with special interest the developments in sport in that country, which he saw as Czarist Russia for the first time in 1912 following the

Olympic Games in Stockholm. There were at that time few sports installations there really suitable for contests. It was here, too, that he broke his right wrist in a contest held under primitive conditions. He found a totally different situation on his second visit in 1934. He was amazed to find that this country had a program for the all-round development of young sportsmen's physical, psychological and ethical values which laid special stress on a broad program of sports. On his third trip in 1954, his visits to sports halls and sports fields convinced him that this program was really underway. And at the 59th IOC Session in Moscow in 1962 Brundage said of the Soviet Union, with frank admiration: "No other country applies more intensively the theory of Baron de Coubertin that a national program of physical training and competitive sport will build stronger and healthier boys and girls and make better citizens."

It is easy to see that the broad development of Soviet sport mentioned by Brundage has brought forth fruit in the shape of the successes and medals won by Soviet athletes at the Olympic Games.

Brundage also pays close attention to the development of sport in the smaller countries. In 1965 he attended the first African Games in Brazzaville (Congo) at which nearly thirty African countries competed. He expressed his appreciation of the fact that here, in a country with less than half the population of the city of Chicago, all the necessary installations were available for these games, which were organised with outstanding success under IOC patronage. He welcomed the admission to the Olympic family of countries which had hitherto taken little part and were not even mentioned in the international sports movement.

All this shows that Brundage tries to correlate the internationalism of the Olympic Games with the efforts of each country to develop its sports movement. Like Coubertin he sees in national effort the basis for international sport. That is why he is always interested in what the separate National Olympic Committees are doing or leaving undone. He draws attention to the dynamic idea of international friendship and strict observance of the Olympic Charter and stresses his conviction that the Games are a genuine source of inspiration towards the idea of peace. Developments have not, of course, always corresponded to these high hopes.

This emerged especially in connection with the conduct of the 1936 Olympic Games, which had been entrusted to the city of Berlin by the IOC in 1932, before Hitler seized power. In the honest belief that these Games, too, could contribute to peace and international friendship Brundage, as president of the United States Olympic Committee championed participation by US athletes, although there were serious differences of opinion about this in the USA because of Hitler's racial laws. The promise, however, given by fascist Germany in connection with the racial problem to the IOC and to the US Olympic Committee was to prove null and void immediately the Games were over.

It is a dark chapter in history that, four years later, Berlin did not bring the Olympic banner entrusted to it by Los Angeles, the city in which the Games were held in 1932, to Helsinki, where the IOC had decided the Games of the XII Olympiad were to be held. The Second World War started from German soil in 1939. It took the lives of countless competitors in the Olympic Games who had faced each other in peaceful contest and deprived many other young athletes of the chance to take part.

Avery Brundage has never concealed his attitude towards war and has repeatedly stated that for him peace is an integral part of the Olympic idea. He regards wars as useless and the expenditure of money on armaments and warlike activities as senseless. He has often pointed out that the USA had to spend 677 thousand million dollars more than its peacetime budget in the two world wars. He stresses what a blessing it would have been for the American people if these huge sums could have been used for peaceful purposes, especially on the education of young people and for amateur sport.

This is a general truth. What vast sums would in fact be available for progress in all fields of human life—to ban hunger in countries which still suffer want, for education, for the arts and sciences, research and so on—if war were finally abolished and the production of nuclear and chemical weapons of destruction stopped.

Brundage's Olympic activities are founded on the firm conviction

17

that further peaceful development of the nations must be based on high ethical values. Brundage agrees with Coubertin's hopes of peace in this higher philosophical evaluation of the Olympic idea—hopes of peace which are nurtured by the growth of character-forming values in the young people taking part in all Olympic Games. Coubertin, in a Message to Youth from Olympia in 1927, said: "In the modern world, full of potent possibilities but at the same time menaced by perilous pitfalls, the Olympic idea can constitute a school of nobility and moral purity as well as of endurance and physical energy, but only on condition that you elevate your conception of honour and self-forgetfulness in sport to the heights of your muscular fitness. The future depends upon you."

Brundage has expressed similar ideas in his speeches and urged that strenuous efforts be made to have these principles put into practice. The measuring of strength between friends who help each other to achieve the best results is a worth-while human task, Brundage believes. Coubertin expressed a somewhat similar view in the introduction to his memoirs:

"What is most important in life is not victory but the struggle; the essential thing is not to have won but to have fought well. To spread these ideas is to make mankind more valiant, stronger—and therefore more conscientious and more generous."

Avery Brundage is guided in his thought and actions by this principle of sportsmanlike courage and fairness. He said in his speech at the opening of the Olympic Winter Games in Cortina d'Ampezzo in 1956:

"The Olympic code of fair play and good sportsmanship, a modern adaptation of the Golden Rule, is observed today on all five continents. One of the objectives of the Olympic Movement is to make these laws of fair play, largely unwritten, so universally accepted that they will be adopted also in other fields. One of the greatest sources of trouble today is the lack of understanding in human relationships. No activity does more to dissipate this lack of understanding than the Olympic Movement. Only when the business and the politics of the world are governed by the same spirit of fair play and good sportsmanship will mankind be able to live in peace."

18

For Brundage the individual competitor is the real backbone of Olympic sport. He once explained his preference for track and field athletics by saying that it was here that individual skill and superiority could be demonstrated.

"The track athlete stands or falls on his own merits," he said. "A boy may be the best football player on the field and still be on the losing team, but the fastest runner usually wins the race, and the most skilful jumper takes the gold medal."

But he does not in any way underestimate the value of team games like football, baseball, basketball and handball, which he himself enjoyed playing for many years. He is recognised as a "Leader-in-Volleyball" in the United States. He said of this game, the inclusion of which in the Pan American and Olympic Games he enthusiastically advocated: "Volleyball is an excellent game for all ages and both sexes, is inexpensive to play and to organize and is perhaps the only truly amateur team sport at an international level in the world."

Again and again Brundage measures up the position in the Olympic Movement against the ideals he has in mind—the ideals which Coubertin had already tried to get put into practice.

"Where do we stand at this time?" he asks. "Have the visions of Coubertin been realized? Should we, who have inherited his ambitious plans, be satisfied? The answer is *no*. Despite the tremendous progress and the extensive accomplishments of the last 70 years the Olympic Movement stands only on the threshold. It has a long way to go to occupy the exalted position which it merits in world society. In only a few countries is it recognized in intellectual, in business or in political circles as an important part of the cultural life." It is therefore logical that Brundage has a particularly high opinion of those countries in which sport is recognised and encouraged by state and society as a determining factor in life.

Avery Brundage is consistently in favour of maintaining the purity of the amateur idea. Along with his sport efforts the Olympic athlete should give his main attention to vocational training and further education, so as to have a firm foundation in life. The problem of amateur status is as old as the modern Olympic Games themselves. Coubertin had already had to take it into consideration in working out the Statutes at the end of the 19th century. He speaks in his memoirs of his efforts to define the term amateur in a definitive way. His successors in the Presidency, the Belgian Count Baillet-Latour (1925–1942) and the Swede Sigfrid Edström (1946–1952) also had to deal with the problem in ever-recurring debates at a variety of IOC Sessions. Although views on amateurism have changed in the course of the years and new definitions have been formulated to accord with developments, no thoroughly satisfactory solution has yet been found.

Once an active amateur sportsman himself, Avery Brundage expends much time and energy on the problem of amateur status and speaks about it at almost every IOC Session. He knows the difficulties, but he is tireless in putting forward his views and has often faced a barrage of criticism because of them. He has occasionally been called "the last of the amateurs," but he has pointed out that there are ten thousand amateurs who engage in sport for sport's sake, for diversion, for recreation, and for fun, to every professional who makes sport a business and participates for money. He is not against professional sport in itself, which in his eyes has the same rights as any other profession—as acrobats in a circus, for example. But he cannot tolerate any mixture of amateur and professional sport which is not sport at all, but business. The extent to which Brundage is concerned with maintaining the purity of the Olympic idea can be seen from a lawsuit conducted against a French sports magazine in 1959. The magazine had published an article headed "The Olympic Flag is the Symbol of a Lie" in which the author accused the IOC and President Brundage of closing an eye to many violations of amateur status. Brundage brought an action for slander against the magazine which aroused considerable interest in the sporting world. He paid all the costs of the court proceedings and he won his case. The magazine had to apologize and disassociate itself from the article in a public statement. For Brundage it was entirely a matter of defending the Olympic ideal, so that winning the case was of fundamental importance to him. He framed the cheque for the symbolic 1-franc damages received and it still hangs in his Chicago office.

Avery Brundage is also opposed to all commercialisation of sport, and he believes that when a sport becomes part of the amusement business it is no longer possible to keep it amateur at the Olympic level and it should be dropped from the program.

Modern championship sports make demands which, apart from occasional surprising natural talent, can only be met if peak sportsmen get sufficient free time for training and contests—for example, a certain period of time to get accustomed to a strange climate. Although Brundage clings to the unadorned simplicity of pure amateur sport, he knows how to take into account the fact that time does not stand still. In his 8oth birthday speech he talked humorously about his youth. There is a tinge of resignation in what he says, but his conclusion is realistic and contemporary: "You had to have a lot of self-reliance in those days and when I think of the pampered athletes of today, with their coaches and trainers, their doctors and nurses, their masseurs, and barbers, and chefs, and psychiatrists, I must say the world has changed."

It is to be hoped that in the interests of the Olympic Movement an answer will be found for amateur problems which accords with our times and takes into consideration the special features of the various Olympic sports. Avery Brundage wants the International Federations and National Olympic Committees to cooperate and reach solutions which will serve further to develop the amateur idea, and thus also the Olympic Movement.

A VERY BRUNDAGE, the successful builder and sportsman who has been connected for decades with the world Olympic Movement, is also a well-informed artlover. Few people are aware of the fact that he has built up and made available to the public one of the largest and probably the most valuable private collection of Oriental art existing today. Following the ideals of antiquity and of the great Frenchman Pierre de Coubertin, he has for many years thought of art and sport in very close juxtaposition.

We have learned that he gained a valuable insight into the nature and history of art through his additional studies as a young man. He smiles today at the way in which people made fun of him for his unprofitable studies. He realised very early that a man must not only be an expert at his own job; he also needs something to balance this in his free time, hobbies which broaden the outlook and enable him to develop a versatile personality. As a disciplined practical man he concentrates on the visual arts and especially on sculpture. This does not, of course, mean that he ignores other forms of art. It is no secret that Avery's wife shares her husband's interests; she was a singer herself and an expert in everything connected with gardens.

For Brundage art is first and foremost a means of diversion and recreation, but like Coubertin he also sees it an effective means of education and he stresses this in his speeches, drawing attention to the traditions of Greek antiquity.

It is unnecessary to enter into detail here about the extremely important role played by art and intellectual education in the ancient Olympic Games. We need only recall that the Greek gymnasium was both a training place for athletes and a place for discussion. Here poets and philosophers spoke to young people, read from their works and conducted talks on philosophy and art. Only a young man who was thoroughly trained both intellectually and physically was regarded as educated. The Greeks thought that a sound mind could only dwell in a sound, well-formed body. For them beauty and goodness combined were what formed personality.

Brundage has repeatedly pointed out that in ancient Greece sport

22

and art were integral parts of culture as a whole. He would like to see an alliance of this kind achieved today, too, and wants to win young sportsmen throughout the world to this idea. That is why he urges all National Olympic Committees to have their members visit museums and art exhibitions, especially during the Olympic Games. The numerous cultural performances provided at the Games in Rome and Tokyo are not the least important reason why he speaks of them with such enthusiasm. This accorded with the wish he expressed in his speech at the opening of the 57th IOC Session before the Games in Rome:

"... today we need to strengthen the educational, moral and the cultural aspects of the program. Where better can this be done than in Rome, which itself is an artistic treasure house..."

But Brundage wants not only to lead sportsmen to art; he also wants to lead artists to sport. He invites art-lovers and cultural workers to visit sports centres. He would especially like visual artists to work in the sports centres, following the example of antiquity, and paint or model athletes in action. Here the artist first obtains the necessary knowledge of the characteristic details which are to be expressed again in the finished work of art. Only in the sports centre itself is it possible to find the immediate, artistically rewarding model, only here can a valuable work of art dealing with a sports theme be created. Brundage has noticed that artists are very often unable, with the best will in the world, to create a genuine work of art in this field simply because they do not understand the laws of movement in the various kinds of sport. Brundage feels that only partially successful efforts are of no value to sport or to art. "What we need," he says, "are mature works of art by the most gifted artists. These will have their effect on the sports movement and strengthen the Olympic idea just as the sculptures of Phidias and the odes of Pindar once did. For one such perfect work of art can inspire millions of people with the Olympic idea."

In his opening speech at the 59th IOC Session in 1962 Brundage summarised his ideas again and made the following suggestions for expanding the scope of cultural performances:

"In pursuit of our objective of the development of the complete man, perhaps we do not sufficiently stress the Fine Art section of the Olympic program. It is true that, at the Games of the XVII Olympiad, our Italian friends did stage a wonderful display of Sport in History and in Art, and I am sure that, in Tokyo, the Japanese with their sensitive love of beauty will also give attention to this section of the program. Even so, more must be done, in my opinion. Perhaps we should give each participating country an hour to display some interesting cultural activity of which it is specially proud. This need not be a competition but merely a demonstration or exhibition of gymnastics, music, opera, ballet, theatre, folk dances, or some other activity."

Suggestions of this kind have certainly played their part in prompting the organising committee of the Games of the XIX Olympiad in Mexico City to appeal to all National Olympic Committees to take part in an art and cultural program as well as in the sports events. These Games will, as a result, be an international festival of athletic, intellectual and artistic value which corresponds to Brundage's ideas.

We must bear these views on the nature and educational role of art in mind in our appreciation of Avery Brundage as an art-lover and collector. He began collecting in 1912. He has said that at first he collected mementos somewhat indiscriminately in the countries he visited—mainly as an active sportsman. He made his first purchases during a tour of Europe which he made after competing in the 1912 Olympic Games in Stockholm. An all-too modest remark which Brundage made later probably refers to these purchases; he said that he had travelled about a great deal and had developed the habit of collecting souvenirs. At first he had not selected things because he thought they were particularly valuable but rather because he wanted to have something characteristic of the country he was visiting.

Decisive for Brundage, who had already taken an interest as a student in Oriental philosophy and art, was a visit to the famous exhibition of Chinese art in Burlington House in London in 1935. What he saw there cast him forever under the spell of East Asiatic art. Since he was never content to do things by halves, Brundage decided to collect

24

systematically from that time on, and in a field in which a collector in the mid-20th century could expect to achieve some completeness. For although, from the point of view of the Olympic idea, collecting works of Graeco-Roman art would have been the more obvious thing to do, it would at that time have been a project doomed to failure. The important works of that period had long been in the possession of museums and other art institutions. Brundage did possess a few works of Greek and Roman art, however, until his house was burnt down. None of these were saved, unfortunately.

As a result of a number of favourable circumstances, China offered a broad field for the collector, especially in the 1930's. Interest had shifted to China when its many-thousand-year-old culture was rediscovered through the exposure of burial sites during the building of the railways. Large quantities of art objects had come to light which, to the astonishment of experts, were found to go as far back in origin as 1500 B.C.

A trip to Japan and around the world in 1939 further encouraged Brundage in collecting Asiatic art. He himself says that it was at this time that he began to devote himself seriously and systematically to building up his valuable collection. As a lover and collector of Oriental art he did not confine himself to China and Japan, however, but later included objets d'art from other great Asiatic cultures—from Korea, Thailand, Cambodia, India and Iran. In the course of time he steadily enlarged and improved his collection, replacing certain items by other more important pieces when available. He still collects today although really outstanding pieces of Asiatic art are becoming more and more difficult to obtain. As a collector he has a sharp eye, made sharper by many years of practice. He has gradually become an expert himself in distinguishing between genuine pieces and later imitations. He tests each newly acquired piece himself and when in doubt relies upon experts working with him. He once remarked humorously that collecting independently meant making mistakes and learning from them, and that he had learned plenty since some forgeries in the field of Oriental art were a thousand years old and very special care had to be exercised.

An expert of the calibre of the late Charles F. Kelley, curator of Oriental art at the Chicago Art Institute, said in praise of Brundage's specialised knowledge: "It would be difficult to deceive him now in the field of Chinese bronzes."

The treasures acquired by Brundage on his travels or through art dealer friends found their way first to his two homes in Chicago and Santa Barbara, California. They piled up in storerooms in the La Salle Hotel, too. Visitors describe how every available bit of space was used to house them and how cautiously one had to move about in these improvised museums, for fear of damaging something. Rare Sung dynasty pieces (980–1278) clustered on shelves in unaccustomed proximity to Tang vases, Greek amphorae, Shang bronzes and jewel-encrusted ornamental plates. His offices were also full of treasures. Only Brundage himself could find his way about and concentrate in the midst of this princely confusion. So that notwithstanding his generosity in allowing artists, art institutions, experts and other interested people to see and study the collection, it was clear that things could not remain as they were. The suggestion was made that Brundage should distribute the collection to the main museums in the United States, so as to "make everybody happy." "Everybody but Avery Brundage," was the reply.

So he decided to donate his collection to one city and asked only in return that a suitable and adequate building be provided for it and that experts be put in charge who would be capable of conducting the necessary research and of applying modern principles of operating a museum so as to help visitors to a proper appreciation of works of art. He loyally offered his collection first to Chicago, since he was a trustee of the Chicago Art Institute, but it already had a large similar collection and had no room for 6,000 more objects. His next choice was San Francisco. San Francisco had no tradition in the field of art collections, but the citizens accepted the challenge with great enthusiasm, and under the leadership of Mayor Christopher passed a bond issue of nearly three million dollars to cover the cost of building a new wing on the Memorial Museum in beautiful Golden Gate Park. Here Brundage's collection finally found a home.

It was no accident that Brundage's choice fell upon San Francisco. In his speech at the opening of the new wing of the Museum with his collection of Oriental art on June 10th 1966, he said:

"The principal reason my collection was given to the City of San Francisco was that San Francisco seems to be the gateway to the Orient, and this Fine Arts Museum, with the cooperation of the great educational institutes of this area, already interested in Oriental history, languages, religion, and philosophy, can be developed into an internationally important center of Oriental culture."

He also explained in detail why it seemed to him so important to understand the Orient:

"Almost two-thirds of the entire human race resides in Asia. Three thousand years ago, when most of the world was inhabited by nomads and ignorant tribes, the Chinese of the Shang Dynasty were making those fantastically beautiful bronze vessels you will see tomorrow when the new wing is opened. These objects, with designs as modern as Picasso, are of a technical excellence that cannot be equalled even today, after thirty centuries of scientific and industrial progress."

And the following remarks in the same speech reveal a deep understanding of the important share which the Asiatic cultures have had in the development of mankind:

"Only one hundred years ago there was no San Francisco. Two hundred years ago there was no United States of America. The exciting Khmer room at the Museum, with its exhibit of spectacular sculptures produced a thousand years ago, gives one something to think about. Here are the remnants of an obviously advanced civilisation which must have lasted hundreds of years. They erected great cities and glorious temples, and then five hundred years ago, vanished completely, leaving the handsome structures buried in the jungle, forlorn and empty, inhabited only by apes, bats and lizards. We think in terms of years, Orientals think in terms of generations, or of centuries, and some Indian philosophers even think in terms of five thousand year cycles. The great religions all originated in Asia. The Chinese invented silk, paper, gunpowder, porcelain, printing, and a hundred other things, and had a well developed civilisation when Europe was in the throes of the dark ages and most of America a wilderness, inhabited only by savages. Japan also has had its indigenous civilisation. Taking those features that pleased it from China and Korea, it retired behind its own borders for three hundred years after Hideyoshi's adventures in Chosen (Korea), until it was brought into the world again in 1853 by Commodore Perry."

Brundage wants his collection in San Francisco to serve the same mission of linking the peoples which underlies his championship of the Olympic idea. In his speech he quite clearly and unmistakably condemns the unfair, unworthy and violent methods which colonialism used in Asia through the centuries in pursuit of its economic and political aims. Here he draws the following conclusions:

"The Orientals have no reason to love westerners... It is time to start over, the world has changed, and perhaps here, San Francisco can play a leading role. No one can study the magnificent works of art displayed in this Museum without gaining new respect for the people who conceived and produced them. Most of them are unsigned, the artists, whose work they are, were true amateurs, whose reward was the satisfaction of a job well done. If we want to understand Orientals, we must study their history, their philosophy and their culture...

"This project, therefore, presents a wonderful opportunity for San Francisco and its people to become leaders in a search for the new understanding so desperately needed, for a bridge of international knowledge and respect. Such a bridge will be of incalculable value in promoting trade and commerce which will benefit every citizen in the community, from the most powerful banker to the most humble newsboy... As the Olympic Movement develops international friendship and amity, so can international understanding and respect come from the study of the fine arts. There is no reason that San Francisco, already a favourite city for foreign visitors, cannot, through this Museum project, construct this bridge, which can be as important as those over the Bay and the Golden Gate, and even more significant internationally. This will be San Francisco's contribution to a happier and more peaceful world."

Although from a cultural point of view the West Coast of the United States looks less to Europe than to the Pacific and across to Asia, San

Francisco possessed next to nothing in the field of Asian art—despite its many citizens of Chinese descent. Because of its size, quality and scope, the collection which Brundage donated to the city of San Francisco in 1959 has brought about a fundamental change in this situation. Brundage has in the meantime worked tirelessly to increase the collection; in 1959, when he made his gift, it consisted of 3,000 pieces, but the number has doubled since then. Today the space available is no longer adequate to display in accordance with accepted museum principles anything like all of the 6,000 objects at one time or permanently. Only a fifth of the collection can be shown in the new wing of the de Young Memorial Museum which was built expressly to house it. Professor René-Yvon Lefebvre d'Argencé, curator of the Brundage Collection, gets over this difficulty for himself and for visitors by changing the exhibits periodically. Professor d'Argencé, a well-known Orientalist of French origin, who was formerly curator of the Cernuschi Museum of Chinese Art in Paris and of museums in Hanoi and Saigon, believes in presenting art in a live way. He provides training courses for voluntary museum docents so as to enable them to give visitors expert guidance. Popular pamphlets on the treasures of the collection are published. Under the guidance of the curator, who has ten expert assistants, a beginning has also been made in cataloguing the contents of the collection in a scientific way.

The collection is still being increased by purchases. In this way gaps in the separate fields can be filled. Wherever possible, too, the losses caused by the fire in Santa Barbara in 1964 are being replaced. Brundage had about 1,000 objects in his house there, only 60 of which were saved. The museum staff are encouraging a general study of Oriental culture, especially of Oriental art. Close contacts are maintained with the neighbouring universities—the State College of San Francisco, the University of California in Berkeley and Stanford University—and their staff has increased rapidly, including both Chinese and Japanese art experts.

The most outstanding event so far was undoubtedly the international symposium which was held from August 29th to September 2nd 1966 in connection with the festive opening of the new Avery Brundage wing of the Museum. This was a unique occasion; experts, collectors and art dealers from all over the world were invited to see the collection and hear lectures on the latest results of research in Asian art. Guests had the opportunity to view in the underground store-rooms works of art which had not yet been exhibited. In a hall specially fitted up for study purposes they were able to inspect countless treasures arranged in glass cases set up in long rows with narrow gangways between. The most prominent Oriental art experts saw here objects of study on which no work had yet been done. It was a memorable occasion when they were permitted to examine closely the ancient Shang and Chou pieces, Han jars, Ming vases, Tibetan bronzes, Khmer and Indian sculpture and glorious examples of Chinese porcelain and jade in Avery Brundage's collection.

Just as broad as the scope of the collection, too, were the subjects of the lectures given at the symposium: Stella Kramrisch spoke on Nepalese sculptures, Jan Fontein on the Buddhist plastic figures in Brundage's collection, Schuyler V. R. Cammann on "A Problem in Chinese Symbolism: the Eight Jewels", and Muneshige Narazaki on Japanese painting about 1600 and the beginnings of the Ukiyo-e style—to name only a few of the most important lectures.

It is hardly possible to express in terms of money the value of Brundage's collection, which has in such a short time attracted the attention of international experts.

The museum building in which the collection has found a home adjoins the beautiful Japanese Gardens in Golden Gate Park. Its wide, high-ceilinged rooms are on three floors. In its outer architecture the wing was a continuation of the Spanish style of the main building, but its interior architecture gives the visitor a sense of bareness and coolness. This has prompted some criticism here and there, but a well-considered principle underlies John Yeon's design. All decoration and elaborateness has been avoided, so as not to allow architectural details to distract people's attention from the museum's contents. The architect has deliberately subordinated himself to the works of art. Visitors must even make some sacrifice in the interests of art, for specific temperatures have to be maintained. Some rooms are kept at a low tem-

30

perature because of the need to abide strictly by rules connected with the preservation of the objects exhibited in them.

The visitor to the museum passes through the entrance into a court-yard which is the centre of the ground floor. Light falls from above. A black marble fountain reveals a special charm when seen in this light-ing. The shape of the fountain gives a first inkling of the museum's specific atmosphere; it is a stylised lotus blossom. The galleries with the exhibition rooms run round the courtyard at the second-story level. The floors are grey, the galleries sparsely lighted, so that bright light falls only on the exhibits themselves. Here and there are win-dows looking out over pine-trees, green hills and the near-by Pacific Ocean.

The first floor houses Chinese art, the second floor the works of other Asian countries (Japan, Korea, Nepal, Persia, India, Thailand, Afghanistan, Vietnam and Cambodia). The exhibits stand out against cool, blue-grey walls. Wall screens and partitions separate the various sections. The fact that a large-scale model was prepared before build-ing began indicates the care with which the interior was planned. Its proportions made it possible to arrange full size experimental replicas of the exhibits and only after the effects produced had been studied were final decisions made on the form and arrangement of glass cases and so on, and on colours and lighting effects.

There is an auditorium for lectures and other proceedings with ac-commodation for 384 persons. Careful attention was paid to the pro-vision of ample rooms with the most modern apparatus for conser-vation work, laboratories with X-ray machines and other special equipment with the help of which damage can be detected before the naked eye can see it. Special baths are provided in which works of art can be expertly cleaned. About 5,000 works which cannot be exhibited permanently in the space available are arranged on the ground floor in such a way as to be accessible to research workers and students.

It is understandable that Brundage takes an active part in the ar-rangement of his section of the museum and in the conduct of it as a whole. He is thoroughly familiar with the practical work of museums since he has been for many years trustee of the Art Institute in Chicago.

It is interesting to note what experts in this field have said about the collection. Here are some comments chosen at random.

Laurence Sickman, curator of the Nelson Gallery of the Atkins Museum in Kansas City, a leading authority on Oriental art, said: "There is good reason to believe that the objects of Asian art offered to San Francisco by Avery Brundage comprise the last comprehensive collection in this field that can be assembled in our time." Some of the pieces, he adds, are unsurpassed. Mr. Sickman says that the early bronzes constitute the largest such collection now privately owned anywhere in the world.

Frank Caro, a well-known New York art dealer and art-lover, who is a friend of Avery Brundage, said of the jade pieces in the collection that they are "the only collection from Shang dynasty (1523–1028 B.C.) to the 19th century with so many examples of each period and type."

It can in fact be said that the collection impresses everybody who sees it, both in its extent and because of the quality of the pieces exhibited. In its variety it surpasses all other private collections of Asian art. It is unique in that a number of pieces in it have never been shown to the international public. It offers experts objects of study for research work for a long time to come.

It is not possible in this short survey to provide anything approaching a complete picture of the Avery Brundage Collection. It contains so many and such a diversity of objects that any attempt at a detailed description must, as Laurence Sickman remarked, be "reduced either to a mere listing of numbers by categories or to vague generalisations about Oriental cultures and their art." Only a few brief remarks will therefore be made which, with the illustrations and Professor d'Argencés expert comments on some of the finest objects, give some impression of the scope and abundance of the collection.

Chinese art, with over 3,000 separate pieces, at present makes up the greater part of the collection. Amongst these are 1,500 examples of ceramics from all important epochs, right back to the Neolithic, jade work from three millenia, 600 archaic bronzes, 200 sculptures in stone and bronze from the 4th to the 18th century which reflect the entire history of Buddhism in China, and 200 pieces of handicrafts, including splendid examples of ivory, lacquer and cloisonné.

The Japanese collection comes second with 500 pieces. Here ceramics occupy first place; these provide a comprehensive survey of the development of Japanese pottery art. In addition there are 130 paintings, including 50 scrolls, and 45 sculptures in wood, lacquer and bronze.

There are 300 examples of handicrafts, especially pottery and metal work, from Korea, and also some excellent specimens of porcelain, lacquer and Buddhist gold-bronze work.

A further 300 pieces come from India, Pakistan and Afghanistan. These include temple sculptures, reliefs, steles, bronze plastics, ivory and wood carvings, which illustrate the main features of Buddhist, Jain and Hindu plastic art of the Indian subcontinent through 1500 years.

Kashmir, Tibet, Nepal and Mongolia are represented by 260 pieces, of which there are 120 gilt bronzes of great iconographic variety; there is also an extensive collection of 17th and 18th century temple banners (Thankas). 150 pieces come from Southeast Asia; here Thai and Khmer sculptures occupy a special place.

This survey should not be concluded without some reference to unusual and unique objects which, like the famous bronze rhinoceros, have won a special place in Avery Brundage's heart. There are, in addition, the hundreds of jade pieces whose grace and smoothness will delight everyone who has pleasure in the play of light on substance, colour and form. He has also collected many small objects, like Japanese tsuba or sword guards, inro and netsuke, small hand-carved wooden or ivory objects, some not much longer than a thumbnail, which served as toggles to anchor the seal and perfume boxes that Japanese gentlemen hung from their kimono sashes.

Brundage once spoke at a meeting of diplomats, functionaries of the Olympic Movement and sportsmen about this hobby of his. He has several thousand netsuke in his collection, all of them ancient, and he held a couple of them in his hand as he spoke. "Originally, these netsuke were carved with loving care for personal use," he said. "The carver conceived the design and built something of himself into the object. It may have taken him six months, but... it bore the stamp of

33

his own personality. He was an amateur carver. Later, after the demand for netsuke grew, there arose a class of professional carvers. These men were usually more accomplished and expert... their work was perhaps more polished and displayed a superior technical skill. But it was ordinarily cold, stiff, and without imagination... Missing was the love and devotion of the amateur carver, which causes these older netsuke to be esteemed more highly by the collector than the commercial product carved for money."

This meeting was in Japan, a country that understands and practices Olympic principles, and the audience was particularly appreciative of this analogy. It was another illustration of Brundage's theory that success in any field comes only to those who have the devotion of the amateur and his search for perfection.

AVERY BRUNDAGE'S life and achievements in the course of the years have met with varying degrees of sympathy and approval. History will show what aspects of his work for the Olympic Movement are of lasting value.

He found a system of ideas and plans for the Olympic Movement already worked out by Pierre de Coubertin in long years of philosophical study. In our modern world, torn by deep-rooted contradictions, it was and is his task as President of the International Olympic Committee to maintain and carry forward this work inspired by the idea of equality, peace and international understanding.

THE SPORTSMAN

1 Avery Brundage's Parents   2 At the Age of Five

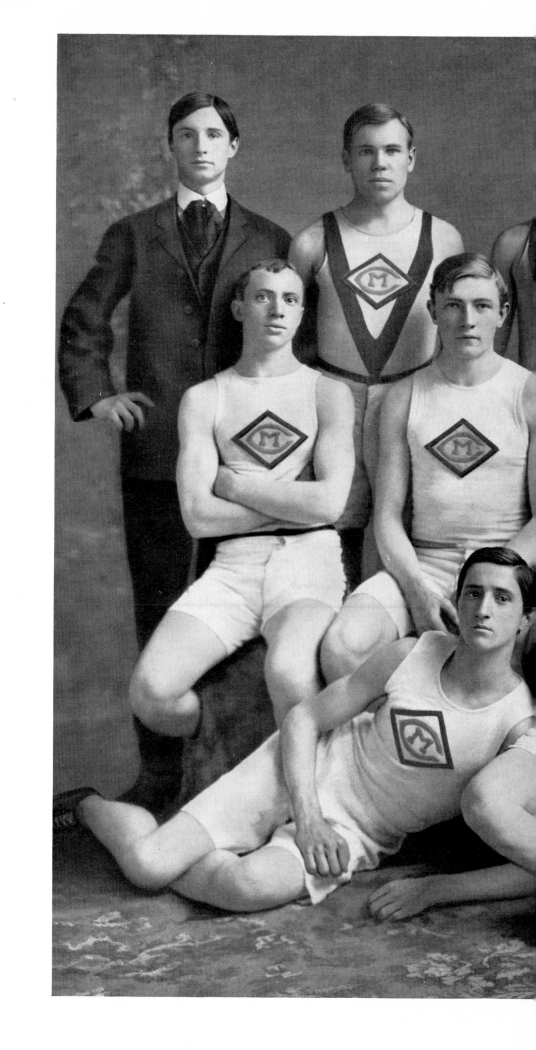

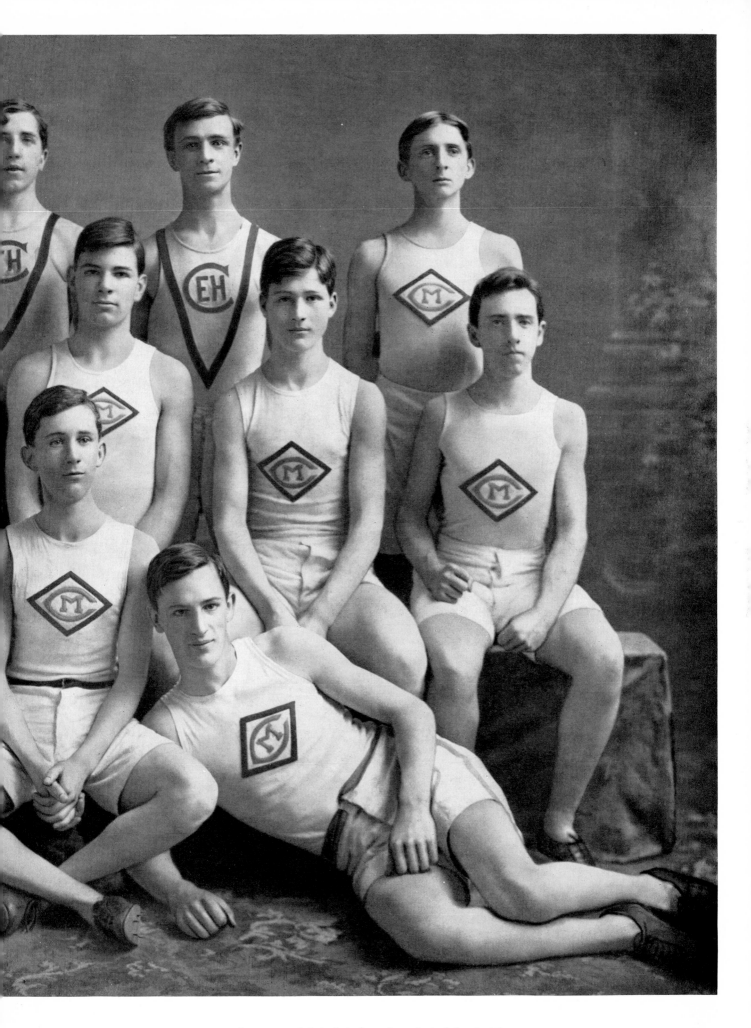

3 Avery Brundage and his high school Athletic Team, 1905

4 In 1909

5 In US Olympic Uniform, 1912

6 Pentathlon Participation Diploma, Stockholm, 1912

7 Participants in the US All-Around Championship, 1916

8 The 100 yard Race

9 The Shot put

THE WORLD MAGAZINE

AND STORY SECTION

SUNDAY, OCTOBER 1, 1916.

AMERICA'S ALL-AROUND CHAMPION

And His Stringent Rules for Athletic Success

No smoking   No drinking
No late hours
Two hours exercise daily
Eight hours of sleep
All the fresh air possible.

AVERY BRUNDAGE, a Chicago contractor twenty-nine years of age, recently captured for the second time the all-around athletic championship of the United States. This does not mean that Brundage is individually the swiftest runner, the highest or broadest jumper or the greatest weight-thrower in the country; but that his average proficiency in all these sports combined is beyond that of his rivals. His victory was achieved by a score of 487 points over his nearest competitor.

This remarkable athlete stands a shade over 6 feet in height, weighs 195 pounds, and since graduation from the engineering school of the University of Illinois he has devoted all his spare time to athletics. He is now in the contracting business on his own account and is in the open air most of the day. From May until October he puts in two hours every night exercising under the moon and stars. In winter the same two hours are spent in a gymnasium where he varies his routine by playing a great deal of handball. Though a speedy runner and a great walker, the events in which he excels are shot-putting and hammer and discus throwing, and these are his favorite sports.

In a life so strenuous as the champion's there is no time left over for diversion, so it is not astonishing that Brundage is still a bachelor.

10   As US All-Around Champion, 1916

11 Walking

12 The Hammer throw

THE MASTER-BUILDER

13 In 1919

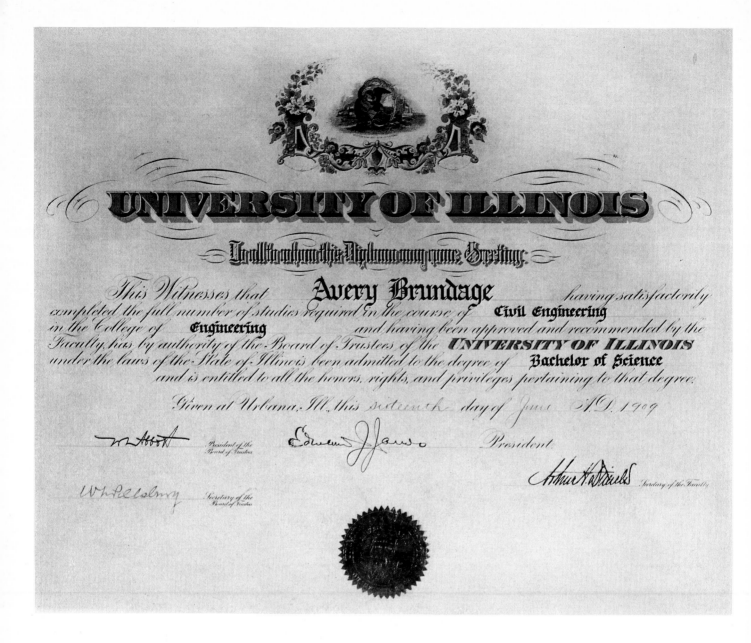

AveryBrundageCompany-
General Contractor

Chicago

15   Avery Brundage Company Brochure title page

16 The Lake Shore Drive, Chicago's "Gold Coast"

17 1448 Lake Shore Drive

18 Shoreland Hotel

19 5000 East End Avenue

ON HIS WAY TO THE PRESIDENCY
OF THE INTERNATIONAL OLYMPIC COMMITTEE

20   Opening Ceremony, Games of the VIII Olympiad, Paris, 1924

21 Diploma, Games of the VIII Olympiad, Paris, 1924

22   Arrival of the US Olympic Team in Amsterdam, 1928

23 Avery Brundage greets Olympic Champion Lord Burghley

24 Reception by Franklin D. Roosevelt, III Olympic Winter Games, Lake Placid, 1932

25 Opening Ceremony, Games of the X Olympiad, Los Angeles, 1932

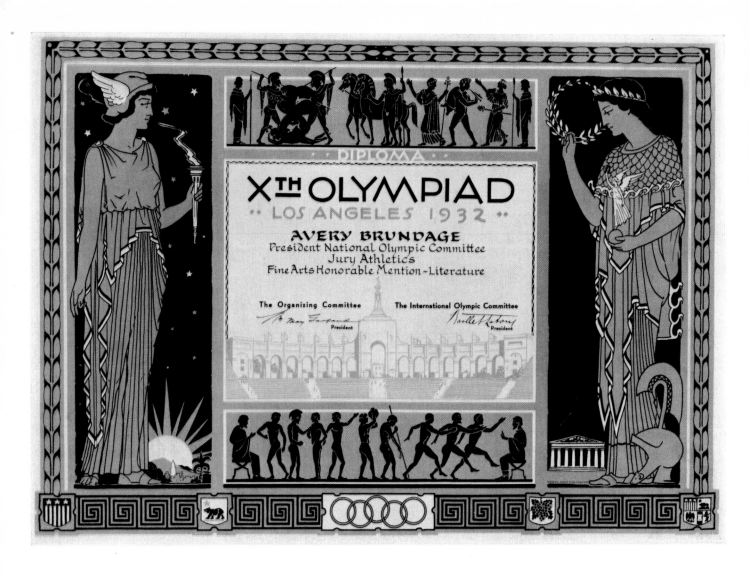

26 Diploma, Games of the X Olympiad, Los Angeles, 1932

27 Count Baillet-Latour on his 60th Birthday with J. S. Edström and Avery Brundage

28 Opening Ceremony of the Games of the XI Olympiad, Berlin, 1936

29 Jesse Owens and Lutz Long: a Friendship broken by the War

30 39th IOC Session, Lausanne, 1946

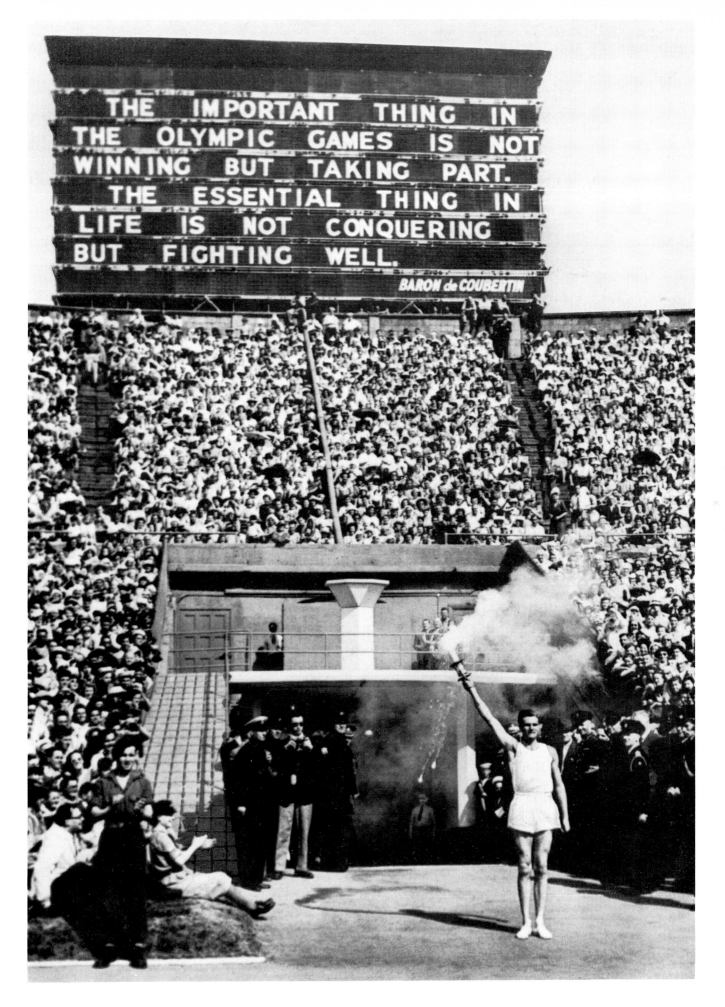

31 Arrival of the Olympic Torch at the Games of the XIV Olympiad, London, 1948

32 45th IOC Session, Vienna, 1951

33 VI Olympic Winter Games, Oslo, 1952

34 At the Head of the US Team, Helsinki, 1952

AS PRESIDENT

OF THE INTERNATIONAL OLYMPIC COMMITTEE

35 J. S. Edström hands over the Key of "Mon Repos" to newly elected President

36 IOC Executive Committee Session, "Mon Repos", Lausanne, 1953

37 Opening Ceremony, VII Olympic Winter Games, Cortina d'Ampezzo, 1956

38 Closing Ceremony, Equestrian Games of the XVI Olympiad, Stockholm, 1956

39 Opening Ceremony, Games of the XVI Olympiad, Melbourne, 1956

40 In Iran for Olympic Day 1956, he visited Persepolis

41   At the Pergamon Museum, Berlin, 1957

42   53rd IOC Session, Sofia, 1957

43 Visiting an Art Exhibition, Tokyo, 1958

44 Victory Ceremony, VIII Olympic Winter Games, Squaw Valley, 1960

45 Opening Ceremony, Games of the XVII Olympiad, Rome, 1960

46 Olympia, 1961

47   Opening 59th IOC Session, Moscow, 1962

48 Presentation of a Bust of Pierre de Coubertin, "Mon Repos", 1963

49 Opening Ceremony, IX Olympic Winter Games, Innsbruck, 1964

50 Opening Ceremony, Games of the XVIII Olympiad, Tokyo, 1964

51　The grave of Pierre de Coubertin, 1965

52 IOC Executive Committee with the International Sports Federations, Lausanne, 1965

53 63rd IOC Session, Madrid, 1965

54 Audience by Pope Paul VI in the Vatican, 1966

55 Opening Ceremony, 65th IOC Session, Teheran, 1967

56 At Mexico City Airport

57 Inspecting construction work, University Stadium, Mexico City

AT HOME IN SANTA BARBARA

58 First Home in Santa Barbara, California

59   A View of Montecito near Santa Barbara

60 The Fire which destroyed his Home, 1964

61 The New Home in Santa Barbara

62 Guests in the New Home

THE FRIEND AND PATRON OF THE ARTS

63 Entrance to the Avery Brundage Asiatic Art Collection, San Francisco

64 The Opening Day

65 A fine arts discussion

66 Ceremonial wine vessel — bronze — China

67 Ceremonial wine vessel — bronze — China

68　Ceremonial food vessel — bronze — China

69 Ceremonial wine vessel — bronze — China

70 Rhinoceros-shaped ceremonial wine vessel — bronze — China

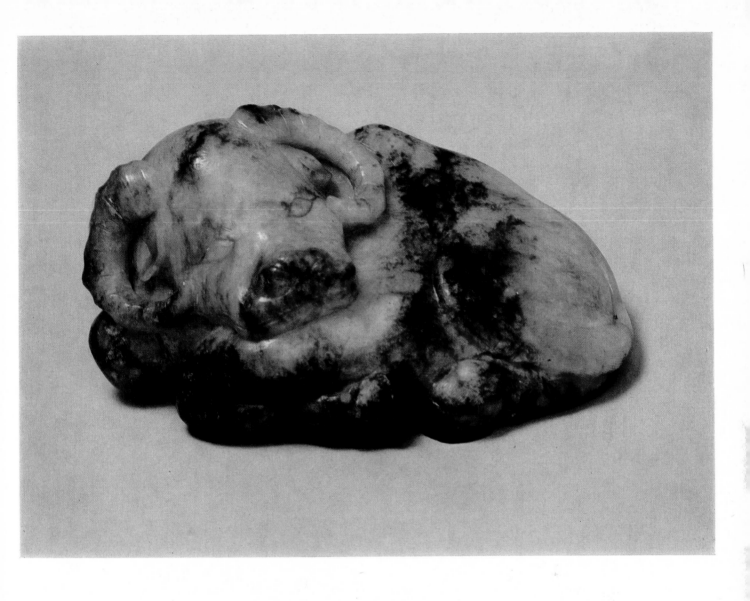

71 Jade Buffalo — China

72 Jade vase — China

73 Lapis Lazuli Mountain — China

74 Vessel — painted pottery — China

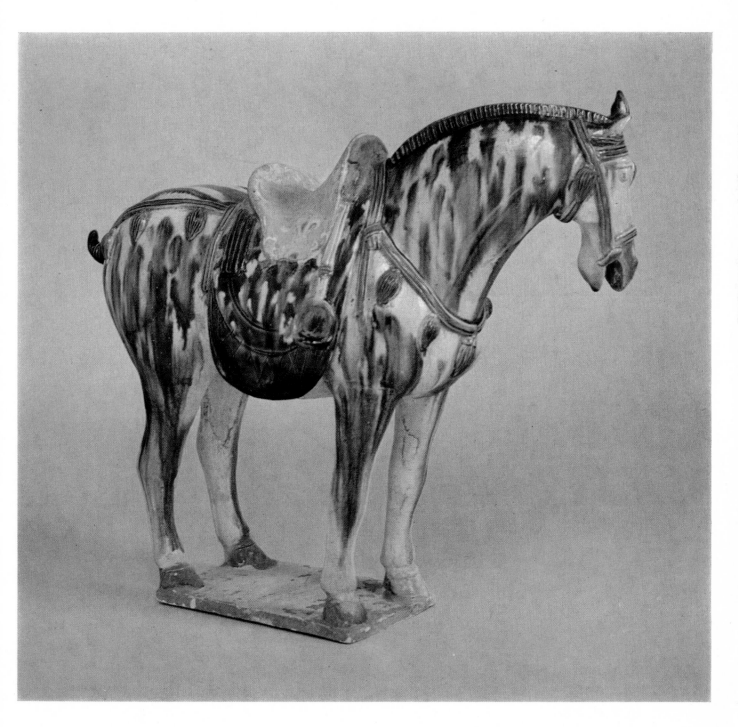

75 Glazed pottery horse — China

76 Celadon cup-stand — China

77 Celadon wine pot — Korea

78 Celadon water dropper, tortoise shape — Korea

79 Porcelain vase with red underglaze — China

80　Jar — glazed stoneware — China

81 Porcelain vase — Famille Verte — China

82 Cosmetic box — lacquer — China

83 Ivory statuette, God of War — China

84 Cloisonné vase — China

85 Box — basketry and lacquer — China

86 Seated Buddha — gilt bronze — China

87 Buddhist Triad — stone stele — China

88 Limestone head of Buddha — China

89 Gilt bronze statuette of Buddha — Korea

90 Wooden statue of a Guardian — Japan

91 P'u-hsien Bodhisattva — wood — China

92 Fugen Bodhisattva painting on silk — Japan

93 Landscape on paper by K'un-ts'an — China

94 Landscape on silk by Yüan Chiang — China

95 "Three Laughing Friends" — painting on paper by Kao Ch'i-pei — China

96 One of a pair of screens by Unkoku Togan — Japan

97 One of a pair of "Southern Barbarians" Screens — Japan

98 Jar — earthenware — Japan

99 Haniwa Clay Warrior — Japan

100 Porcelain platter — Japan

101 Red sandstone torso of Buddha — India

102 Schist relief representing Maya's Dream — Gandhara

103 Granite statue of Brahmani — India

104 Black chlorite Buddhist stele — India

105 Bronze statue of Kaliya Khrishna — India

106 Bronze statue of Lokeshvara — Thailand

107 Lava stone head of a Dhyani Buddha — Java

108 Sandstone statue of Vishnu — Khmer

109 Sandstone statues of a Royal Couple — Khmer

110 Battle of Monkeys — red sandstone lintel — Khmer

111 Gilt bronze torso of Buddha — Thailand

112 Eleven-headed Aryavalokiteshvara — bronze — Kashmir

113 Gilt bronze statuette of Samvara — Tibet

114 Goddess Lhamo — painting on silk — Tibet

115 Pottery stag — Iran

116 Pottery plate — Iran

AT THE HEIGHT OF HIS CAREER

117 Another journey for the Olympic Movement

118 The La Salle Hotel Chicago

119 A Host of Birthday Guests

120 Reading Birthday Greetings

121 General José de J. Clark F. conveys the Congratulations of IOC Members

122   Douglas F. Roby, President US Olympic Committee, brings congratulations

123 Talking with Jesse Owens

124 Conversation with old friends

125 With fellow workers at his hotel

LIST AND EXPLANATIONS
OF ILLUSTRATIONS

contributed to the skyline of the city of Chicago.

16 View of Lake Shore Drive, the "Gold Coast" of Chicago. Here the Avery Brundage Company built several of the sky-scrapers which can be seen in the picture.

17 Apartment house on Chicago's "Gold Coast", built by the Avery Brundage Company in 1926

18 Shoreland Hotel, built by the Avery Brundage Company in 1925. When it was built, this was one of the largest and finest hotels in Chicago.

19 One of the apartment houses on East End Avenue built by the Avery Brundage Company in 1928

20 Opening ceremony, Games of the VIII Olympiad, Paris, 1924. 3,092 athletes from 44 countries competed in these Games.

21 Avery Brundage's diploma from the Games of the VIII Olympiad in Paris. Below, to the right, Pierre de Coubertin's signature. Brundage was a member of the US Olympic Commitee. The magnificent Finnish runner Paavo Nurmi was the outstanding athlete at these Games.

22 The US Olympic team arriving at Amsterdam docks to take part in the 1928 Olympic Games. 3,015 athletes from 46 countries took part in these Games.

23 Avery Brundage greets the 1928 Olympic 400 m hurdles victor, David Lord Burghley (now Marquess of Exeter), in Chicago in 1930. The meeting took place on the occasion of the US – British Empire track and field athletic contest. Lord Burghley had previously taken part in the British Empire Games in Hamilton, Ontario (Canada).

24 Reception on the occasion of the III Olympic Winter Games at Lake Placid, 1932, given by Franklin D. Roosevelt, at that time Governor of New York State and later US President. In the background, to the left beside the two-branch chandelier, the then President of the IOC, Count Baillet-Latour; below the Olympic rings between two ladies, Franklin D. Roosevelt; extreme foreground, Avery Brundage

25 Opening ceremony of the Games of the X Olympiad, 1932 in the Los Angeles stadium. 1,408 athletes from 37 countries took part in these Games. Sportsmen where accommodated for the first time in an Olympic village specially built for them.

26 Avery Brundage's diploma of participation as President of the US Olympic Committee at the Games of the X Olympiad, Los Angeles, 1932. Below to the right, signature of Count Baillet-Latour, IOC President

27 IOC President Count Henri de Baillet-Latour on his 60th birthday in 1936, with his successors. From left to right: Count Henri de Baillet-Latour (President 1925–1942), J. Sigfrid Edström (President 1946–1952), Avery Brundage (President since 1952)

28 Parade of Nations at the opening of the Games of the XI Olympiad in Berlin, 1936. 4,069 athletes from 49 countries took part in these Games. The outstanding athlete was the American Negro Jesse Owens. He won four Gold Medals — in the 100 m race (10·3 sec.; Olympic and world record), 200 m race (20·7 sec.; Olympic record), long jump (8·06 m; Olympic record) and as participant in the 4×100 m relay race (39·8 sec.; Olympic and world record), thus disproving fascist racial theories before the whole world.

29 Jesse Owens and Lutz Long, the two great rivals in the long jump at the Games of the XI Olympiad in Berlin, 1936, winners of the Gold and Silver Medals. They became close sports friends in Berlin, remembering the five interlaced Olympic rings which symbolise the links between the nations and race. Both hoped to meet again at the 1940 Olympic Games. This hope was dashed by the war in which Lutz Long, like other Olympic competitors of many nations, lost his life. A splendid sign of the permanency of the friendship begun in 1936 is the fact that Jesse Owens still corresponds with Lutz Long's son.

30 First IOC Session after the Second World War, in Lausanne in 1946 under the chairmanship of its President J. S. Edström (right). The Syndic and later Mayor of Lausanne, Pierre Graber (left),

expresses his thanks for the Olympic Cup, awarded to the city by IOC for the year 1944.

31 After a journey of thousands of miles, the Olympic Torch arrives in London's Wembley Stadium for the opening of the Games of the XIV Olympiad in 1948. There was a record number of competitors at these Games—4,689 athletes from 59 countries.

32 45th IOC Session, Vienna, 1951. Erik von Frenckell (Finland) speaking. In the Presidium beside President J. S. Edström, Vice-President Avery Brundage

33 Avery Brundage in the stadium for the VI Olympic Winter Games in Oslo, 1952. He escorts Princess Ranghild of Norway to the opening ceremony. 732 sportsmen from 30 countries took part.

34 In his capacity as President of the US Olympic Committee, Avery Brundage leads the American athletes into the stadium for the opening of the Games of the XV Olympiad in Helsinki, 1952. 4,925 athletes from 69 countries took part. The most important event here was the participation of Soviet sportsmen in the Olympic Games for the first time. The Soviet athletes were the most successful in these contests. Outstanding were Soviet gymnast Victor Chukarin, who won four Gold Medals, and Emil Zatopek of Czechoslovakia, who won three Gold Medals; his wife also won the Gold Medal for throwing the javelin.

35 Before the memorial to Coubertin at "Mon Repos," IOC headquarters in Lausanne, Avery Brundage as newly elected President of IOC receives the official keys from the hands of his predecessor J. S. Edström on August 15th 1952.

36 IOC Executive Committee Session under the chairmanship of its President Avery Brundage in "Mon Repos," IOC headquarters in Lausanne, 1953. From left to right: Dr. Miguel A. Moenck (Cuba), Armand Massard (France), President Avery Brundage (USA), Otto Mayer, IOC Chancellor (Switzerland), Lord Burghley (now Marquess of Exeter, Great Britain), Prince Axel of Denmark

37 Opening ceremony of the VII Olympic Winter Games in the newly-built icestadium in Cortina d'Ampezzo, 1956. These games, in which 924 sportsmen from 32 countries competed, were the first to be conducted under Avery Brundage's Presidency. For the first time in the history of the Olympic Games a woman spoke the Olympic oath. The outstanding competitor was the Austrian Anton Sailer, who won three Gold Medals.

38 Closing ceremony of the Equestrian Games in Stockholm, 1956, which because of the complicated Australian import regulations for horses were not held in Melbourne but in Stockholm as part of the Games of the XVI Olympiad. 159 sportsmen from 29 countries took part in these Games. Here IOC President Avery Brundage hands over the lowered flags to the Lord Mayor of Stockholm.

39 At the Opening of the Games of the XVI Olympiad in Melbourne, 1956. 3,184 athletes from 67 countries took part. Extreme left, the Duke of Edinburgh, who opened the Games on behalf of the British Queen Elizabeth, beside him Kent Hughes, President of the Organising Committee, then Australian Prime Minister R. G. Menzies and Avery Brundage

40 In 1956 Avery Brundage visited the ruins of Persepolis, capital of the old Persian Empire destroyed in 330 B.C. This was an instance of the great interest which he always shows in ancient cultures.

41 Avery Brundage paid a visit to the NOC of the German Democratic Republic in 1957 on his way to the 53rd Session of IOC in Sofia. Here he not only visited sports stadiums and halls in Berlin, but also the world-famous Pergamon Museum. Here, beside IOC President Avery Brundage, Heinz Schöbel, President of the NOC of the GDR

42 53rd IOC Session in Sofia, 1957. To the right of Avery Brundage, Colonel-General Vladimir Stoytscheff, President of the NOC of Bulgaria and Member of IOC

43 During the 54th IOC Session in Tokyo, 1958, Avery Brundage visited a special exhibition of Oriental art at which some valuable pieces

from the Avery Brundage Collection were shown.

44 Avery Brundage paying tribute to the 500 m women's speed–skating victors at the VIII Olympic Winter Games, Squaw Valley, California, 1960, in which 665 sportsmen from 30 countries competed.

45 Opening ceremony of the Games of the XVII Olympiad in the Stadio Olimpico, the Stadium of the 100,000, in Rome in 1960. Carrier-pigeons fly off to all parts of the world. 5,337 athletes from 84 countries took part. The Games surpassed all previous ones in participation and in achievements. 29 world records and 71 Olympic records were established or improved.

46 After the 58th IOC Session in Athens in 1961 the IOC, together with representatives of international sport, visited Olympia, where the stadium excavated in recent years by the German Archaeological Institute in Athens was handed over to the Greek Ancient Monuments Administration.

47 Avery Brundage speaking at the opening ceremony of the 59th IOC Session in the immense new Congress Hall of the Kremlin in Moscow, 1962.

48 In honour of the 100th birthday of Pierre de Coubertin (1.1.1963) Dr. Heinz Schöbel, President of the NOC of the German Democratic Republic, presented a bust by the Berlin sculptor Wieland Förster of the founder of the modern

Olympic Games at "Mon Repos." Left to right: Vice-President Armand Massard, President Avery Brundage, Dr. Heinz Schöbel, Helmut Behrendt, Secretary-General of the NOC of the GDR, Jan Weymann, Secretary-General of the NOC of Switzerland, and Otto Mayer, Chancellor of IOC

49 Avery Brundage opens the IX Olympic Winter Games in the Bergisel Stadium in Innsbruck, capital of Tyrol, Austria, before 60,000 spectators. 1,111 sportsmen from 36 countries took part—a record for the Winter Games.

50 Opening ceremony of the Games of the XVIII Olympiad, the first to be held in Asia, in Tokyo with its ten million inhabitants, in 1964. 5,558 athletes from 94 countries took part—again a record participation. The Olympic Torch was kindled before 80,000 spectators in the National Stadium by the 19-year-old student Josainori Sakai, who was born near Hiroshima on August 6th 1945 — on the very day on which the bomb fell on Hiroshima.

51 Avery Brundage pays homage to the founder of the modern Olympic Games, Pierre de Coubertin: a visit to Coubertin's grave during a session in Lausanne in 1965.

52 IOC Executive Committee Session with the International Sports Federations, April 12/13th 1965. Representatives of 25 international sports Federations attended the session.

53 Avery Brundage with members of the Executive Committee during a working session of the 63rd IOC Session in Madrid, 1965

54 Pope Paul VI receives members of IOC in the Vatican on the occasion of the 64th IOC Session in Rome, 1966. In an eloquent speech he expressed interest in physical education and sport.

55 Opening ceremony of the 65th IOC Session in Teheran, 1967. The Shah of Persia delivering his speech. In the foreground, beside Avery Brundage, Fara Dhiba, the wife of the Prince Gholam Reza Pahlavi

56 Avery Brundage paid several visits to the Organising Committee of the Games of the XIX Olympiad in Mexico City in 1966 and 1967 to see how the preparations were progressing. Architect Pedro Ramírez Vázquez, President of the Organising Committee of the Games, showed him the extensive building operations and gave him an idea of the tremendous efforts, which the Mexican people are making to ensure that the Games will be a new climactic point in the Olympic Movement. In the picture, beside Avery Brundage, left, Architect Pedro Ramírez Vázquez; right, IOC Vice-President General José de J. Clark F.

57 Inspecting construction work in the University Stadium in Mexico City, the scene of the opening of the Games of the XIX Olympiad in Mexico City, 1968.

58 Avery Brundage's first home in Santa Barbara, the coastal city northwest of Los Angeles, California, which was built as a Spanish outpost in 1782.

59 View of Montecito near Santa Barbara, which enjoys the mild climate of California. The ocean, the green coastal belt, and the enclosing mountains give this park-like landscape its special charm. In the centre, the Montecito Country Club, which Avery Brundage owns and operates.

60 In September 1964 a huge forest fire spreading down from the mountains reached the Santa Barbara region. Despite the use of aeroplanes and the efforts of more than 1,000 fire-fighters, it was impossible for a considerable time to get the fire under control. Avery Brundage's house was one of the victims.

61 Avery Brundage now has a new home not far from the one which was burnt down.

62 Members of the IOC Executive Committee in Mexico City for the 2nd International Sports Week, accompanied by IOC Secretary-General J.W. Westerhoff, accepted Avery Brundage's invitation to visit Montecito. From left to right: Ivar Emil Vind (Denmark), General José de J. Clark F. (Mexico), Avery Brundage, Sheikh Gabriel Gemayal (Lebanon), J. W. Westerhoff, Dr. Giorgio de Stefani (Italy)

63 Entrance to the Avery Brundage Art Collection in San Francisco. The collection found a home in a new

184

wing, specially built for it, in the Memorial Museum in San Francisco's Golden Gate Park. It was handed over by Avery Brundage at a ceremony on June 10th 1966, as a gift to the city of San Francisco.

64 A number of prominent San Franciscans and outstanding experts and art lovers showed their deep appreciation of the exhibition when they went through the new rooms after the opening of the museum.

65 Avery Brundage talking with Professor Yvon d'Argencé (centre), Director of the Avery Brundage Foundation, and Roger Broussal, Conservator of the Collection.

66 Ceremonial wine vessel, bronze, green patina with azurite and malachite encrustations. China. One-character inscription cast on bottom of receptacle. 13—11th century B.C. Late Shang period. H: 14—3/4 in., Diam: 6–3/4 in. Some 3500 years ago metallurgy was introduced into China, thus marking the beginning of a remarkably long-lived and luxuriant Bronze Age. This monumental vessel ranks among the largest to have been excavated from the Chinese soil. It probably belonged to members of a royal family who used it in ceremonies honoring the spirits of their ancestors.

67 Ceremonial wine vessel, bronze, rich yellowish patina with brown patches. China. 13–11th century B.C. Late Shang period. H: 13-3/4 in., Diam: 6–3/4 in. After spending many centuries in tombs where they were in contact with various soil chemicals or other objects, ancient Chinese bronzes have developed colorful patinae which can be very appealing to the Western eye. The surface decoration of this bottle-shaped vessel exemplifies one of the central motifs of Shang art. This is a frontal mask with bulging eyes known as t'ao-t'ieh. Frequently made of two dragons facing each other it also suggests a blending of feline and bovine prototypes.

68 Ceremonial food vessel, bronze, green patina with heavy malachite encrustations, one-character inscription on bottom. China. 13–11th century B.C. Late Shang period. H: 14 in., Diam: 9-1/2 in. Whether they were used for the offering of food or wine, many types of ancient Chinese bronze vessels stand on three cylindrical, conical or triangular legs. These, however, are rare examples of fully zoomorphic legs. Shang Bronze Art is essentially animal art. In those early days birds rarely occupy a central position but they frequently appear as secondary or auxiliary motifs.

69 Ceremonial wine vessel, bronze, dark brown patina, similar inscriptions cast on bottom of container and back of lid. China. 11–10th century B.C. Late Shang or Early Western Chou period. H: 12-1/2 in., L: 15 in. This massive specimen illustrates a category of syncretic vessels which appeared towards the end of the Shang dynasty. Their

stylistic development was dominated by audacious combinations of quadrupeds and birds but also included reptiles and even human elements.

70 Ceremonial wine vessel in the shape of a rhinoceros, bronze, brownish black patina pitted with greyish-green and red patches. A 21-character inscription is cast on the bottom. China, ca. 11th century B.C. Late Shang period. H: 9 in., L: 13 in. This unique vessel is also one of the most celebrated items in the Avery Brundage Collection regardless of age, provenance and medium. As a collector's item its history can be traced back to 1843 when it was excavated in Shantung province near Confucius' birthplace. Quite a few ancient Chinese bronze vessels bear cast inscriptions. This one, unusually lengthy for the period, refers to a gift of cowries made by the king to a high official on the occasion of a sacrifice commemorating a successful expedition. The beast conveys a sense of latent ponderous energy, almost of a suspended motion which is typical of Shang animal art at its best.

71 Recumbent buffalo. Greyish-green jade with black and brown markings. China. 206 B.C.-A.D. 220. Han dynasty. L: 7-3/8 in. The compact contours of this ruminant are derived from the natural shape of a small boulder. The massive head has a squared-off muzzle and large, fluted horns resembling those of a ram. Bold incisions mark the facial features and the hooves, which are executed all around.

72 Vase. Dark green jade. China. Dated 1789 A.D. Ch'ing dynasty, Ch'ien Lung period. H: 18 in., W: 9-1/2 in. The shape and surface decoration of this thick-walled vase are largely derived from those of archaic bronze vessels. The long inscription on the neck is filled in with gold paint.

73 Mountain. Lapis Lazuli with off-white markings. China. 18th century. A.D. Ch'ing dynasty, Ch'ien Lung period. H: 9-1/4 in., W: 13 in. Chinese lapidaries did not pay much attention to lapis Lazuli prior to the 18th century A.D. This is a scene of Taoist inspiration where an Immortal and his servant collect the fungus of immortality in a mountainous landscape setting.

74 Funerary pottery. Grey stoneware with "birdicized" clouds painted in red, white and indigo with red outlines. China. 3rd–1st century B.C. Western Han dynasty. H: 23 in., Diam: 16 in. This vase is a faithful replica of a contemporary bronze vessel and served as an inexpensive substitute for burial purposes.

75 Figure of a horse. Funerary pottery. Buff earthenware with a three-color glaze showing streaks of blue, amber and brown. China. 680–750 A.D. T'ang dynasty. H: 14-3/8 in., L: 18 in. The horse is shown in a typical attitude with its head turned sideways and its four legs firmly planted on a rectangular base.

76 Cup-stand. Porcelain covered with translucent olive green glaze. China. 11th–12th century A.D. Sung dynasty. H: 7 in., Diam: 7 in. An unusual and particularly fine example of the earliest types of porcelain ever produced in China and in the world. The carved decoration on the lip and the reticulated body reveal a high degree of technical achievement.

77 Porcelain wine-pot with celadon glaze. Korea. 11th–12th century A.D. Koryo period. H: 9–5/8 in., Diam: 6–1/2 in. Korean potters produced celadon wares which have proven to be equal if not superior to those of their Chinese counterparts.

78 Water dropper in the shape of a dragon-headed tortoise. Porcelain with celadon glaze. Korea. 11th–12th century A.D. Koryo Period. H: 3–1/2 in., L: 4 in. Such zoomorphic containers were probably made in fairly large quantities to be used on the scholar's desk but very few specimens have survived.

79 Porcelain vase with underglaze red decoration. China. 14th century A.D. Yüan dynasty. H: 18 in., Diam: 9 in. Decoration in red or blue painted on a porcelain body marked the beginning of the pictorial phase of Chinese ceramics.

80 Jar. Stoneware with turquoise, blue, aubergine and yellow glazes applied to the biscuit according to the "cloisonné" technique. China. Circa 1500 A.D. Ming dynasty. H: 18 in., Diam: 14 in. The main panel shows the mythical Eight Immortals of Taoism paying court to Shou Lao, the God of Longevity.

81 Porcelain vase decorated in Famille Verte enamels. China. Ch'ing dynasty. K'ang-hsi period (1662–1722 A.D.). H: 30 in., Diam: 9 in. The Famille Verte group is a technical triumph which marked the full maturity of the decorator's palette. The central ornamental scheme depicts in rich colors an audience at the camp of a Manchu high dignitary.

82 Lacquer Cosmetic Box with painted decor and metal fittings. China. Dated 218 B.C. Ch'in dynasty. H: 7 in., Diam: 4–3/4 in. The use of lacquer from very early times was a Chinese monopoly. This container bears on the outside geometric designs painted in red on a black ground.

83 Ivory Figurine of Kuan Ti, the God of War. China. 15th century A. D. Ming dynasty. H: 11 in. The God is shown sitting on a high chair in a very theatrical posture probably inspired by scenes of the classical Chinese opera.

84 Vase. Cloisonné enamel with gilt-bronze mounts. China. 16th century A. D. Ming dynasty. H: 21–1/8 in., Diam: 11–1/4 in. The decor consists of tense floral scrolls in red, yellow and white against a turquoise ground. The dragon-shaped "handles" are later additions probably dating from the 17th or 18th century.

85 Box. Lacquer with basketry panels. China. Early 17th century A.D. Ming dynasty. H: 4-3/4 in., L: 19 in., W: 13-1/2 in. The lid is topped by a large rectangular panel showing a meeting of high officials in a partly architectural, partly natural setting. The scene is painted in brilliant colors outlined in gold on a black ground.

86 Gilt Bronze Buddha. China. Dated 338 A.D. Posterior Chao dynasty. H: 15-1/2 in., W: 9-5/8 in. This Buddha seated in meditation on a high rectangular platform is the earliest dated piece of Chinese sculpture known.

87 Stone Buddhist Stele. China. Dated 533 A.D. Northern Wei period. H: 67 in., W: 30 in. Buddha and attendant Bodhisattvas stand in high relief against an ebullient background of figures and floral motifs in low relief.

88 Limestone head of Buddha from the Lei-ku-t'ai cave at Lung-men. China. Circa 700 A.D. T'ang dynasty. H: 26 in. This head belonged to a monumental statue which occupied the central place in a cave of the eastern sector of Lung-men. It shows all the characteristics of the T'ang style at its apex.

89 Gilt Bronze Buddha. Korea. 8th to 9th century A.D. Great Silla dynasty. H: 19 in. This statuette ranks among the largest and earliest Korean buddhist effigies outside of Korea. Derived from Chinese prototypes of the T'ang period, it shows pronounced Korean characteristics such as the heaviness of the head, the squatness of the body and the sternness of the facial features.

90 Guardian King. Wood with traces of gesso and color. Japan. Late 9th century A.D. Early Heian period. This fierce yet youthful effigy was carved in one piece of wood with the exception of the upper part of the headdress which is a later addition. Like most guardians of the period this one probably stood on a gnome whose deformed body he was crushing under his feet.

91 P'u-hsien Bodhisattva. Wood with traces of polychromy. China. Circa 14th century A.D. Yüan or Early Ming dynasty. The crowned Bodhisattva of Benevolence is sitting in erect position, one leg flexed on a kneeling elephant, his usual vehicle. The right hand holds a scroll, possibly representing the 26th chapter of the Lotus Sutra which was devoted to P'u-hsien.

92 Fugen Bosatsu (Bodhisattva). Color and cut gold on silk. Japan. 13th century A.D. Kamakura period. H: 25 in. Fugen is the Japanese transliteration of P'u-hsien (see No.91). Here the Bodhisattva is shown as a princely deity riding a six-tusked white elephant in a cloudy paradise. Her hands are joined in the attitude of prayer.

93 "The River Bend". Ink on paper. Dated 1661 A.D. By K'un-ts'an. China. Ch'ing dynasty. H: 39-1/2 in., W: 47-1/4 in. K'un-ts'an spent most

of his life in seclusion and the bulk of his work reflects an ebullient if somewhat pent-up sensibility which could only express itself when in close contact with nature. The dense explicitness of the landscape, far from being static, is animated by a sweeping movement based on firm rhythmical brushstrokes.

94 Landscape. Ink and colors on silk. Dated 1707 A.D. By Yüan Chiang. China. Ch'ing dynasty. H: 7–3/8 ft., W: 45–1/8 in. In the foreground of this vertical tripartite composition a rocky promontory projects into a wide river. The rocks shelter a mansion consisting of several one-story buildings. These architectural elements are depicted in a precise, delicate manner which contrasts vividly with the bold if studied brushwork of the rest of the painting.

95 "Three Laughing Friends". Ink and color on paper. By Kao Ch'i-pei. (Ca. 1672–1734 A.D.). China. Ch'ing dynasty. H:71 in., W:20 in. The commonplace theme of scholars looking at a waterfall is treated in a highly original manner. Kao Ch'i-pei created striking effects by using his hand, fingers and nails instead of the conventional brush.

96 "The Hermitage". One of a pair of screens. Ink and color on paper. By Unkoku Tōgan (1547–1618 A.D.). Japan. Momoyama period. H: 65 in., W: 150 in. Tōgan claimed to be the spiritual heir of the famous 15th century artist Sesshu who was large-

ly responsible for the introduction of Chinese-inspired ink monochrome landscapes in Japan.

97 Section of Namban Byōbu or "Screens of the Southern Barbarians". Ink and colors on gold-leafed paper. Japan. Ca. 1600 A.D. Late Momoyama or Early Edo period. H: 68–1/4 in., W: 131 in. Some forty examples of such screens are still extant. They depict with a profusion of brilliant colors and humoristic touches the arrival of Jesuit priests and Portuguese traders in Nagasaki and Sakai during the second half of the 16th century.

98 Earthenware jar. Japan. 3rd millennium B.C. Jōmon culture. H: 17 in. This type of pottery was made throughout the Japanese neolithic period for over 4000 years. It reveals that the innate sense of Japanese potters for sculptural effects has a very long history.

99 Haniwa Warrior. Japan. 5th–6th century A.D. Old Tomb period. H: 40 in. This low-fired clay warrior in full armour stands erect on a barrel-shaped cylinder. The sculptor has typically achieved lively effects with remarkably economical means. The eyes and mouth are simply gouged out and only essential details like the riveting of the helmet, the shoulder trappings and the gauntlets are rendered realistically.

100 Ko-Kutani Platter. Porcelain decorated with green, yellow and aubergine enamels. Japan. 17th century A.D. Early Edo period.

189

Diam: 13 in., H: 3-1/4 in. This unusually large dish typifies the boldest type of Japanese enameled wares. The main features of the Ko-Kutani production are figurative themes illustrated in thick brilliant colors standing against a white background and delineated by crisp brushstrokes.

101 Red sandstone torso of Buddha from Mathura, India. 2nd century A.D. Kushan dynasty. H: 20-1/2 in., W: 13-1/2 in. Although Buddha was born some twenty-five hundred years ago his effigy did not appear in Buddhist art until about seven centuries later. This fragment of a standing statue belongs to the earliest representations of Buddha in India proper.

102 Schist relief representing Maya's Dream. Gandhara. 3rd century A.D. H: 10 in., L: 11-3/8 in. This is the illustration of a famous scene when Buddha's mother, Maya, dreamed that a white elephant, symbolizing the future Buddha, was entering her body through her right side. Early Gandharan workshops were largely inspired by contemporary Roman provincial art.

103 Granite statue of Brahmani. South India. 9th century A.D. Chola period. H: 29 in. This three-headed, four-armed statue shows Brahma, the central figure of the Hindu Trinity, in his feminine form. The deity is seated cross-legged on a low, semicircular pedestal. In the front of the pedestal between the deity's feet the swan Hamsa, Brahma's vehicle, is shown in low relief.

104 Black chlorite Buddhist Stele. Bengal, India. 10th–11th century A.D. Pala period. H: 41 in. A crowned Buddha stands in clinging, transparent garments below a parasol with a stupa-shaped point. The Buddha holds a lotus flower in his left hand and is flanked by four diminutive Buddhas. This stele typifies the work of Bengali sculptors who were the only ones to remain faithful to Buddhism in post-Gupta India.

105 Bronze statuette of Kaliya-Krishna. Sundaraperumalkoil. Tanjavur district. South India. 15th century A.D. Vijayanagar period. H: 27 in. Krishna, in Hindu mythology one of the incarnations of the Solar God Vishnu, was of Herculean strength even as a child. Here he is shown squeezing and trampling Kaliya the Serpent-Demon to make him promise he will leave the waters of the river.

106 Bronze statue of Lokeshvara. From site near Prakornchai. Northeastern Thailand. 7th century A.D. Chenla period. Lokeshvara "The Lord of All the Worlds" stands in frontal posture with its legs slightly apart. His four arms terminate in lotus-shaped hands holding detachable attributes. The chignon is decorated with loops and a diminutive effigy of Buddha Amitabha, thus

showing a blending of Hindu and Buddhist mythology. This is one of the earliest Khmer bronze sculptures so far discovered.

107 Lava stone head of a Dhyani Buddha. From Borobudur. Java. Ca. 800 A.D. Shailendra dynasty. H: 12 in. This head was originally located in one of the numerous niches which embellish the terraces of Borobudur, a gigantic stupa portraying in stone the cosmic system of Mahayana Buddhism.

108 Grey sandstone statue of Vishnu. Cambodia or Northeastern Thailand. Ca. mid-10th century A.D. Pre Rup style. H: 56 in. This is the image of a well-fed, prosperous and slightly distant monarch who was also worshipped as a god. Sculpted shortly after Angkor became the capital of the Khmer empire, it illustrates the typically Angkorean concept of the God King. Characteristic of the style are the soft if somewhat overpowering smile, the straight nose, the mustache which curves up without undulating and the pronounced eyebrows forming a continuous sharp ridge across the high forehead.

109 Veined sandstone statues of a Royal Couple. Cambodia or Northeastern Thailand. Late 11th century A.D. Baphuon style. H: 44 and 41 in. The royal figures probably personify the Hindu deities Shiva and his spouse Parvati since the male figure bears the third eye of Shiva on the forehead. They were made at a time when Khmer sculptors yielded to an ideal of feminine beauty and contrast vividly with the virile Vishnu of the previous plate.

110 Red sandstone Lintel illustrating a Battle of Monkeys. Cambodia or Northeastern Thailand. 11th–12th century A.D. H: 35 in., L: 74 in. Hanuman, Sugriva and their army of monkeys play an important part in the Ramayana, an ancient Indian epic poem which tells the adventures of Rama, one of the incarnations of the God Vishnu.

111 Gilt bronze Torso of Buddha. Thailand. 15th century A.D. Early Ayuthia style. H: 22-1/8 in. This elegant figure with its distant but serene expression was cast at a time when Thai sculptors were beginning to develop a style of their own. As one would expect from a transitional piece it retains a number of features which are usually associated with earlier styles such as the shape of the ear and the pronounced curvature of the sharp nose ridge.

112 Statuette of an eight-armed, eleven-headed Aryavalokiteshvara. Bronze with silver inlay, faces are gilt and hair painted blue. Kashmir. 11th century A.D. This is one of the most popular representations in lamaist Buddhism which held its sway over Tibet, Nepal and Kashmir for many centuries. Avalokiteshvara, the spiritual son of the Buddha Amitabha is shown with

eleven heads arranged pyramidally as a symbol of the deity's boundless compassion. The topmost head is that of Amitabha himself.

113 Gilt Bronze statuette of Samvara. Tibet. 17th century A.D. H: 12 in. The most potent of the tutelary divinities of Lamaism are those who act conjoined with their shakti or feminine energy. Samvara has twelve arms and four heads. Among his attributes are fragments of elephant hide, an axe, a cup made of a skull and a thunderbolt.

114 Painting on silk (Tanka) representing the Goddess Lhamo. Tibet. 17th century A.D. H: 40-3/4 in., W: 27-1/4 in. Numerous temple banners were painted by lamaist monks and believers as an act of piety. They usually record the complexities of lamaist iconography and a few display real artistic talents. Lhamo is the most frightening of a group of Eight Terrible Divinities. She was armed by all the gods as being the most ardent defender of the doctrine of Buddha.

115 Rhyton in form of a Stag. Dark Brown baked clay. Amlash. Iran. 10th–8th century B.C. H: 11-3/8 in. Amlash art and the corresponding culture were totally unknown less than forty years ago. Today excavated materials include pottery with often anthropomorphous or zoomorphic vessels, bronzes and jewels. In Amlash animal art

lively postures are blended with abstracted forms in a manner which looks strangely familiar to the modern eye.

116 Bowl. Minai ware, overglaze painted in red, blue, black and gold on a white ground. Iran. Early 13th century A.D. H: 3-3/4 in., Diam: 6-1/2 in. This type of enameled ware was produced during the last decades of the 12th century and the beginning of the 13th century in a region centering on Kashan and Rayy. Decorators yielded to the "miniature" taste as exemplified by this scene showing a seated prince with two attendants amidst foliate patterns and bird designs.

117 As President of the International Olympic Committee Avery Brundage must take long journeys throughout the world.

118 In the La Salle Hotel in Chicago, which belongs to him, Avery Brundage celebrated his 80th birthday on September 28th 1967 with prominent Chicago citizens and officials and friends from all over the world.

119 A host of birthday guests

120 Reading the birthday greetings which reached Avery Brundage from all parts of the world on his 80th birthday. To the right of the speaker's desk, Avery Brundage and his wife

121 IOC Vice-President General José de J. Clark F. (Mexico) conveys to Avery Brundage the congratu-

192

lations of IOC members. He presented a silver platter on the back of which are engraved the names of all IOC members.

122 Douglas F. Roby, President of the US Olympic Commitee and member of the IOC, brings Avery Brundage the good wishes of his National Committee and hands him a gift.

123 Among the guests who came to congratulate Avery Brundage on his 80th birthday was the winner of four gold medals at the Games of the XI Olympiad in Berlin 1936, Jesse Owens, with his wife.

124 Talk with old friends centred round preparations for the Games of the XIX Olympiad in Mexico City in 1968. Left to right: IOC Vice-President General José de J. Clark F., Pedro Ramírez Vázquez, President of the Organising Committee of the Games of the XIX Olympiad in Mexico City (partly concealed), Douglas F. Roby, President of the USOC and Member of IOC, and Kenneth L. Wilson, former president of the USOC

125 Avery Brundage on his 80th birthday with employees of the hotel, who have worked with him for many years.

126 On his 80th birthday Avery Brundage was in the limelight on television, radio and press.

BIBLIOGRAPHY

Books and articles

Bushnell, Asa S. (ed.), United States 1952 Olympic Book; New York 1953

Coubertin, Pierre de, Mémoires Olympiques; Lausanne 1931

Hartman, Joan M., "The Brundage Collection in San Francisco", Oriental Art, Vol. XIII, No. 2, Summer 1967

Kluge, Volker, Die Olympischen Spiele von 1896–1964; Berlin 1968

Lefebvre d'Argencé, René-Yvon, Chinese Treasures from the Avery Brundage Collection; New York 1968

– "The Asian Wing at the de Young Museum", The Society for Asian Art, Newsletter, Vol. 7, No. 1, May 1967

– The Avery Brundage Collection of Asian Art, Asia Foundation Program Bulletin, Special Issue; San Francisco 1966

Mayuyama, Junkichi, "The Olympic Game of Oriental Arts", Tobi, No. 12, 1967

Mezö, Dr. Ferenc, Sechzig Jahre Olympische Spiele; Berlin–Budapest 1956

Mizuno, Seiichi, "The Brundage Symposium", Jinbutsu-orai-sha, October 1966

Schöbel, Dr. Heinz, Olympia und seine Spiele, 2nd ed.; Berlin–Leipzig 1967

Selz, Peter and Frankenstein, Alfred, "The Brundage Collection", Art in America, Vol. 55, Number Five, September-October 1967

Shaplen, Robert, "Profiles: Amateur", The New Yorker, July 23, 1960

Sickman, Laurence, "The Avery Brundage Collection at the de Young Museum", The Art Quarterly, Vol. XXVIII, Nos. 1, 2, 1965

Sullivan, Michael, "The Avery Brundage Collection in San Francisco", The Burlington Magazine, Vol. CIX, No. 769, April 1967

Weigle, Edith, "The man who has everything", Chicago Sunday Tribune Magazine, July 30, 1961

Olympic bulletins and publications

Bulletin du Comité International Olympique, Nos. 53, 72, 79, 95

The Olympic Games – Rules and Regulations...; Lausanne 1967

The author also used hitherto unpublished documents in the archives of IOC President Avery Brundage

ILLUSTRATIONS

We are grateful to the following for permission to reproduce illustrations in this book:

Archives of IOC President Avery Brundage: 1–19, 21, 23, 24, 26, 27, 33, 34, 40, 43, 46, 47, 51, 54, 58–62, 117–126

M.H. de Young Memorial Museum, San Francisco, California: 63–116

Archives of the National Olympic Committee of the GDR, Berlin: 20, 22, 28, 29, 37, 39, 41, 42, 44, 48, 52, 55

Archives of the International Olympic Committee, Lausanne: 30, 32, 35

Presseagentur Schirner, Berlin: 31, 36, 38

Comité Olímpico Mexicano: 56, 57

Bunte Deutsche Illustrierte Zeitung, Offenburg: 45

Fritz Fenzl, Munich: 49

Spanish Olympic Committee: 53

Spence Air Photos, Los Angeles, California: 25

Sportverlag Berlin: 50